Passing your ITIL® Foundation Exam

London: TSO

Published by TSO (The Stationery Office) and available from:

Online
www.tsoshop.co.uk

Mail, Telephone, Fax & E-mail
TSO
PO Box 29, Norwich, NR3 1GN
Telephone orders/General enquiries: 0870 600 5522
Fax orders: 0870 600 5533
E-mail: customer.services@tso.co.uk
Textphone 0870 240 3701

TSO@Blackwell and other Accredited Agents

Customers can also order publications from:
TSO Ireland
16 Arthur Street, Belfast BT1 4GD
Tel 028 9023 8451 Fax 028 9023 5401

First edition Crown Copyright 2007
Second edition Crown Copyright 2009

First published 2009
Second impression 2011

ISBN 9780113312061

Printed in the United Kingdom for The Stationery Office
P002429127   c25   05/11

Contents

List of figures

List of tables

OGC's foreword

I have never particularly enjoyed the experience of sitting an exam. The anxious build-up, hours spent poring over pages of lengthy text, the intense atmosphere of the examination room. I could go on but I'm sure that most of you have been there at some point in your lives.

The best you can hope for in such a situation is to be well prepared. Study aids are an essential part of this and attending an accredited training course will also provide learning support, often with case studies and examples that can bring the ITIL® framework to life.

Over the years, the content has been further developed and expanded as it incorporates the latest identified best practices. The sheer scope and depth of the complete ITIL Service Management Practices framework can seem daunting as an examination subject.

This publication successfully presents the content in a simplified structure, ideal for learning and developing knowledge. Sadly it won't make you an overnight success in the world of Service Management, but it will certainly point you in the right direction.

The content has been updated to bring it into line with the revised syllabus, and to ensure it reflects the current approach to exam questions. In particular, I commend the case study, which I believe achieves its aim to reinforce, simplify and explain some of the concepts in ITIL that are fundamental to passing the Foundation Exam.

The next step, of course, is to pass the examination. But hopefully it won't seem such a challenge once you've studied this publication.

Best of luck!

Jonathan Shebioba

Director of Best Management Practice

Office of Government Commerce

Chief Examiner's foreword

As the practices of ITIL become further embedded in organizations and the global Service Management industry, the recognition of IT Service Management (ITSM) as a profession grows in acceptance.

The ITIL Qualification Scheme supports the quest for formal knowledge and certification, and these are recognized not only for the Service Management capabilities they engender in the workplace, but also as building blocks for a career path and as a symbol of IT Service Management professionalism.

The ITIL Foundation certificate for Service Management is the first of those building blocks. As part of a larger series of official study aids supporting ITIL qualifications, this publication is intended to help individuals studying the ITIL foundation curriculum and preparing for the exam. It will help students to understand the basics of ITIL Service Management practices and join the growing ranks of recognized Service Management professionals.

Knowledge gained today is the opportunity of tomorrow.

Sharon Taylor
Chief Examiner, ITIL

The Official Accreditor's foreword

The updating of ITIL to this current version has resulted in several new topics being interwoven into the well-known processes and approaches many people are familiar with. ITIL version 3 is documented fully in five volumes – *Service Strategy, Service Design, Service Transition, Service Operation* and *Continual Service Improvement* – which provide detailed advice and guidance for Service Management professionals.

This publication covers the material within the revised version 3 Foundation syllabus (effective from 1 May 2009) and aims to help candidates prepare for their Foundation Exam. It has been reviewed on behalf of the APM Group by Mark Flynn of Felix Maldo Ltd and Gary Hodgkiss of PTS Consulting. It is an excellent companion to course notes and other material provided by accredited training companies.

This publication is endorsed by the APM Group and has itself passed a rigorous assessment process.

We wish you every success with your forthcoming exam and hope you will make full use of the excellent guidance offered here.

Richard Pharro

CEO, APM Group Ltd

Acknowledgements

Chief Architect and author

Sharon Taylor,
Chief Architect

Aspect Group Inc.

Christian F. Nissen,
author

CFN People – formerly:
ITILLIGENCE

Contributors

A number of people generously contributed their time and expertise to this publication. The author would especially like to thank:

- Rosemary Gurney (Wardown Consulting Ltd) for her huge effort in making the language readable and understandable in English
- Lise Dall Eriksen (CFN People) who checked that the study aid publication covers all the topics in the ITIL version 3 Foundation syllabus
- A number of IT Service Management experts, trainers and examiners, including Lars Zobbe Mortensen (Zobbe Consult & Zoftware), Signe-Marie Hernes Bjerke (DNV), Thomas Fejfer (CFN People), Katsushi Yaginuma (ITpreneurs), Majid Iqbal (Carnegie Mellon University), Ivor Macfarlane (IBM), Shirley Lacy (ConnectSphere), Gary Case (Pink Elephant) and Michael Imhoff Nielsen (IBM), for their comments and advice regarding the drafts produced in the development cycle
- Bente Skøtt (OK Gasoline) who read and commented on the final draft as a representative for the target audience of the publication
- Emily Allison and Janine Eves from TSO who have been very supportive in answering questions and providing material and information during the development of the publication.

The Stationery Office would like to thank Michelle Hales (ConnectSphere) for creating some of the sample questions.

The ITIL Qualification Scheme

1

1 The ITIL Qualification Scheme

ITIL (formerly known as the Information Technology Infrastructure Library) is best-practice guidance for IT Service Management, which is used by many hundreds of organizations around the world. A whole ITIL philosophy has grown up around the advice contained within the ITIL books and the supporting certification and Qualification Scheme.

The purpose of the ITIL Qualification Scheme is to ensure that relevant and timely certifications are available to support the formalized learning requirements of individuals and organizations related to the ITIL Service Management practices. This has grown to become the international standard for IT Service Management in providing a common language and set of practices for use throughout the world.

The official ITIL Qualification Scheme is the only training and qualification scheme leading to official ITIL qualifications in IT Service Management.

1.1 LEVELS OF QUALIFICATION

The ITIL Qualification Scheme introduces a learning system that enables an individual to gain credits for all ITIL courses that can be applied towards a recognized professional achievement (Figure 1.1). Once candidates have accumulated a sufficient number of credits, they can be awarded the ITIL Expert in IT Service Management certification.

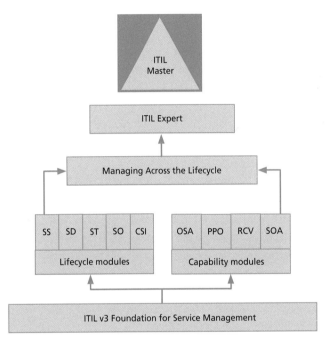

Figure 1.1 The ITIL Qualification Scheme

To achieve the ITIL Expert certification, candidates must obtain a minimum of 22 credits, two of which must be from the Foundation module, which is a mandatory first step, and five of which must be from the 'Managing Across the Lifecycle' module, which is a mandatory final step.

Candidates can choose modules from the Capability (four credits per module) or Lifecycle (three credits per module) streams to gain the other 15 credits, but are expected to choose a balanced programme overall.

1.1.1 ITIL Foundation certificate in IT Service Management

The foundation level offers a general awareness of the Service Lifecycle and the key elements within.

The learning objectives and competencies are focused on an understanding of the overall linkages between the stages in the lifecycle, the processes used and their contribution to Service Management practices.

More details of the ITIL Foundation certificate in IT Service Management can be found in section 1.3.

1.1.2 ITIL Intermediate qualification certificates in IT Service Management

The intermediate level is a dual-stream modular certification series, each with a set of certifications and a normalization certification. The purpose of the certificates is to impart and test detailed knowledge about the contents of parts of the ITIL core publications. The intermediate qualifications are grouped in three sets:

1 The Service Lifecycle stream will be of interest to candidates wishing to obtain knowledge of ITIL practices within the Service Lifecycle context. The prime focus is the lifecycle itself, the use of process and practice elements within it, and the management capabilities needed to deliver quality Service Management practices in an organization. An examination is given for each module

2 The Service Capability stream will be of interest to candidates who wish to be certified in a deep-level understanding of ITIL processes and roles. Attention to the Service Lifecycle is illustrated as part of the

curriculum; however, the primary focus is on the process activities, execution and use throughout the Service Lifecycle. An examination is given for each module

3 The Managing Across the Lifecycle qualification completes the intermediate level and is a capstone qualification for both the Lifecycle and Capability streams.

Both intermediate streams assess an individual's comprehension and application of the concepts of ITIL. Candidates are able to take units from either of the intermediate streams. These units give them credits towards an ITIL Expert certificate.

1.1.2.1 Service Lifecycle

The intermediate Service Lifecycle stream is built around the five ITIL core publications:

1 Service Strategy (SS)

2 Service Design (SD)

3 Service Transition (ST)

4 Service Operation (SO)

5 Continual Service Improvement (CSI).

1.1.2.2 Service Capability

The intermediate Service Capability stream is built around four clusters:

1 Operational Support and Analysis (OSA)

2 Service Offerings and Agreements (SOA)

3 Planning, Protection and Optimization (PPO)

4 Release, Control and Validation (RCV).

1.1.2.3 Managing Across the Lifecycle

Managing Across the Lifecycle (MALC) – a final intermediate course module – brings together the full essence of the lifecycle approach to Service Management. This certification completes the Lifecycle and Capability streams by focusing on the knowledge required to implement and manage the necessary skills associated with the use of the lifecycle practices.

1.1.3 ITIL Expert in IT Service Management certificate

Once a candidate has gained the required number of credits through their education and has successfully passed the required examinations at the foundation and intermediate levels, they will be awarded the ITIL Expert in IT Service Management certificate. No further examination or course is required to gain the ITIL Expert certificate.

1.1.4 ITIL Master in IT Service Management certificate

The ITIL master level will assess an individual's ability to apply and analyse the ITIL concepts in new areas. This higher certificate had not been developed when this publication was released.

Details of the various learning options, certifications and combinations can be found on the ITIL Qualification Scheme website: www.itil-officialsite.com/Qualifications

1.2 QUALIFICATIONS BODIES

This section outlines the roles of the organizations within the official ITIL Qualification Scheme. Candidates should ensure that when buying ITIL training, it is acquired from an ITIL-accredited organization.

1.2.1 OGC

ITIL was originally developed by the UK government organization Central Computer and Telecommunications Agency (CCTA), which in 2000 was merged into the Office of Government Commerce (OGC), an office of HM Treasury.

OGC has established collaborative partnerships with two organizations to provide support for its ITIL portfolio. As the official accreditor, the APM Group provides accreditation services related to examination institutes and training providers, and is responsible for the qualification scheme. The Stationery Office (TSO) is the official publisher of all official ITIL Service Management practices framework publications, including this one.

OGC retains the rights to all intellectual property, copyright and trademarks relating to ITIL. Its predominant role in the official scheme is one of ownership and stewardship of the ITIL library content and qualifications. The APM Group chairs the Qualifications Board (the steering committee made up of representatives from the community who make decisions about qualifications policy) and ensures decisions made are to the benefit of ITIL and users alike.

1.2.2 APM Group

The APM Group is an international professional accreditation and certification body, which is accredited to international standards by the United Kingdom Accreditation Service (UKAS), which ensures the effectiveness, impartiality and quality of APM Group scheme administration services. In 2006, the APM Group became OGC's official accreditor for ITIL and is now responsible for the monitoring and promotion of the official scheme for training, consulting and qualifications.

Within its role as the official ITIL accreditor, the APM Group is responsible for setting the standards and syllabuses throughout the market which any delivering examination institute must adhere to, as well as creating, maintaining and delivering the ITIL Qualification Scheme itself.

The APM Group is also responsible for the accreditation and monitoring of any examination institute applying to the official scheme to run ITIL qualifications and accredit training organizations.

1.2.3 Examination institutes

The APM Group as the official accreditor is authorized to license other examination institutes to administer ITIL qualifications and accreditation activities. Under the contracts signed with the APM Group, examination institutes are allowed to conduct the following activities:

- Approve training organizations
- Administer examinations via those organizations they have approved.

The list of the current examination institutes can be found on www.itil-officialsite.com/ExaminationInstitutes/ExamInstitutes.asp

1.2.4 Accredited training organizations

Accredited training organizations (ATOs), sometimes known as accredited course providers (ACPs), are companies that have been assessed and approved by an examination institute to run officially accredited training courses and administer examinations in ITIL.

These accredited organizations must submit:

- Their quality management systems, detailing their processes for administration of the training courses and examinations

- The course material they use during training ITIL candidates for the examinations
- Their trainers for assessment by an examination institute.

Following approval by an examination institute, ATOs are granted a licence by the APM Group as the official accreditor to use the relevant OGC-owned intellectual property rights and trademarks relating to ITIL.

1.2.5 *it*SMF International

The IT Service Management Forum (*it*SMF) is the not-for-profit international community for IT Service Management professionals, with more than 50 chapters worldwide and a coordinating organization – *it*SMF International. The chapters provide local support to those individuals and organizations using and implementing ITIL.

*it*SMF is recognized as an integral part of the ITIL community. It is a collaborative partner to the ITIL official scheme and participates on the Qualifications Board.

1.3 THE ITIL FOUNDATION CERTIFICATE IN IT SERVICE MANAGEMENT

1.3.1 Purpose

The purpose of the ITIL Foundation certificate in IT Service Management is to certify that the candidate has gained knowledge of the ITIL terminology, structure and basic concepts and has comprehended the core principles of ITIL practices for Service Management.

The ITIL Foundation certificate in IT Service Management is not intended to enable the holders of the certificate to apply the ITIL practices for Service Management without further guidance.

1.3.2 Target group

The target group of the ITIL Foundation certificate in IT Service Management is drawn from:

- Individuals who require a basic understanding of the ITIL framework and how it may be used to enhance the quality of IT Service Management within an organization
- IT professionals who are working within an organization that has adopted and adapted ITIL, who need to be informed about and thereafter contribute to an ongoing service improvement programme.

1.3.3 Prerequisites

There are no formal criteria or prerequisites for candidates wishing to attend an accredited ITIL foundation course, though some familiarity with IT terminology and an appreciation of their own business environment is strongly recommended.

1.3.4 Learning objectives

The learning objectives of the ITIL Foundation certification in IT Service Management are to enable the candidate to:

- Define service and to comprehend and explain the concept of Service Management as a practice
- Understand the Service Lifecycle and how the processes integrate with each other throughout the lifecycle, and explain the objectives and business value for each stage in the lifecycle
- Define some of the key terminology and explain the key concepts of Service Management
- Comprehend and account for the key principles and models of Service Management, and balance some of the opposing forces within Service Management

- Understand how the Service Management processes contribute to the Service Lifecycle, to explain the high-level objectives, scope, basic concepts, activities and challenges for five of the core processes and state the objectives and some of the basic concepts for 13 of the remaining processes, including how they relate to each other
- Explain the role, objectives and organizational structures of the Service Desk function and state the role, objectives and overlap of three other functions
- Account for and be aware of the responsibilities of some of the key roles in Service Management
- Understand how service automation assists with integrating Service Management processes
- Explain the ITIL Qualification Scheme.

1.3.5 Reference

The full syllabus with detailed descriptions of each of the learning objectives can be downloaded from the ITIL website: www.itil-officialsite.com

1.4 ABOUT THIS PUBLICATION

This publication is based on the syllabus for the ITIL Foundation certificate in IT Service Management. It is therefore neither an introduction to ITIL nor a brief summary of the ITIL core publications. Rather, it is a study aid to support the acquisition of knowledge and skills required to achieve the ITIL Foundation certificate in IT Service Management.

One of the foundation learning objectives is to understand the common terminology used within ITIL, and readers may find it useful to access the official ITIL glossary of terms and definitions (see www.best-management-practice.com and navigate to 'Glossaries and Acronyms').

The structure of the publication does not strictly follow the order of the syllabus. Instead it is structured with ease of learning in mind. Basic concepts are introduced in Chapters 2 and 3 ('Introduction to Service Management' and 'ITIL and the Service Lifecycle') to form the basis for the concepts, principles and practices that are introduced in the subsequent five chapters, each representing a core publication. Each of the five core chapters is identically structured to help the acquisition of the covered concepts, principles and practices. The two subsequent chapters ('Service Management technology' and 'How it all fits together') contain transverse topics.

At the end of each chapter a mind map and a number of sample test questions are presented to enable the reader to rehearse and practise the content of the chapter. The number of questions in each chapter corresponds to the typical distribution of questions in an exam.

It is hoped that you will find Service Management enjoyable and you will acquire the new knowledge and skills necessary for achieving the ITIL Foundation certificate in IT Service Management.

Introduction to Service Management

2 Introduction to Service Management

'People do not want quarter-inch drills. They want quarter-inch holes.' Professor Emeritus Theodore Levitt, Harvard Business School

2.1 SERVICES AND SERVICE MANAGEMENT

2.1.1 Services

> Brigitte enters an alpine hotel in a middle-sized town in Switzerland. She is on a short business trip and needs to stay over for the next two nights. She has just got out of the taxi and approaches the hotel reception to ask for a service from the hotel: accommodation.

To understand what Service Management is, we need to understand what services are, and how Service Management can help service providers to deliver and manage these services.

The outcomes that customers want to achieve are the reason why they purchase or use a service. The value of the service to the customer is directly dependent on how well a service facilitates these outcomes.

> **Definition**
>
> A **service** is a means of delivering value to customers by facilitating the outcomes customers want to achieve without the ownership of specific costs and risks.

If you buy an apartment, the ownership of the specific costs and risks are transferred to you as part of the trade. But if you stay at a hotel, the ownership of the specific costs and risks remains with the service provider. The same is the case if you take a taxi instead of buying a car.

> Brigitte has never thought of it in that way. She is going to inspect the production of a medical company tomorrow and the overnight accommodation enables her to start work very early in the morning and it reduces the geographical constraints put on her by living in Denmark.
>
> Brigitte gets a room that satisfies her need to stay overnight without having to undertake the cost and risk of owning her own apartment in Switzerland.

2.1.2 Service Management

Service Management is what enables a service provider to understand the services they are providing; to ensure that the services really do facilitate the outcomes their customers want to achieve; to understand the value of the services to their customers; and to understand and manage all the costs and risks associated with those services.

> **Definition**
>
> **Service Management** is a set of specialized organizational capabilities for providing value to customers in the form of services.

These capabilities include the management practices, processes, functions, roles, knowledge and skills that a service provider uses to enable them to deliver services that create value to their

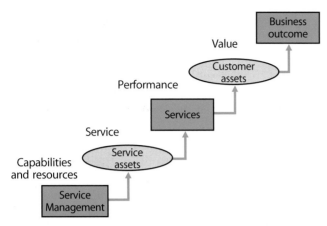

Figure 2.1 Service Management is the art of transforming resources into valuable services by exploiting the organization's capabilities

customers. The capabilities represent their capacity, competency and confidence for action (see section 2.1.6 for a definition of' 'capability'.

The act of transforming resources (Figure 2.1) into valuable services is at the core of Service Management. Without the capabilities, a service organization is merely a bundle of useless resources.

As a service provider the hotel needs to establish functions such as a concierge, reception, kitchen and facilities management as well as processes such as booking, request fulfilment, Capacity Management and cooking. They are all examples of capabilities that help the hotel to transform resources in the form of staff, food and buildings into valuable hotel services.

But the hotel must also ensure that it hires people who have acquired the appropriate level of knowledge and skills through education and experience within the profession.

However, Service Management is more than just a set of capabilities. It is also a professional practice supported by an extensive body of knowledge, experience and skills. A global community of individuals and organizations fosters its growth and maturity.

2.1.3 Service value: utility and warranty

Customers value a service when they see a clear relationship between the service and the business value they need to generate. From the customer's perspective, the business value of a service is created by the combination of two elements (see Figure 2.2):

- **Service utility** What the customer gets – or fitness for purpose
- **Service warranty** How it is delivered – or fitness for use.

Definition

Service utility is the functionality offered by a service from the customer's perspective.

Service utility increases the average performance of customers' assets by improving customers' productivity or outcomes or by removing constraints on their performance.

Definition

Service warranty is the assurance that a service will meet its agreed requirements. This may be a formal agreement such as a Service Level Agreement or contract, or it may be a marketing message or brand image.

Four characteristics of service warranty are that it:

- Is provided in terms of the availability of services
- Is provided in terms of the capacity of services
- Ensures that customer assets continue to receive utility, even if at degraded service levels, through major disruptions or disasters
- Ensures security for the value-creating potential of customer assets.

Warranty decreases the possible losses for the customer from variation in performance. Customers feel more certain that their demand for service will be fulfilled with the same level of utility with little variation.

Customers cannot benefit from something that is fit for purpose but not fit for use, and vice versa. It is useful to separate the logic of utility from the logic of warranty for the purpose of design, development and improvement.

It is the first time Brigitte has been confronted with the concept of utility and warranty. But when she thinks about it, it makes perfect sense.

She looks around. The bed, table and bathroom are good examples of utility in that they fulfil her need for sleep, the ability to work in her room and to have a bath before she leaves for her appointment tomorrow.

But to create value, the room must be available on the night she needs it, there must be internet bandwidth enough for her to prepare for the next day's work on her laptop, and she must feel secure in her room. These conditions are examples of warranty.

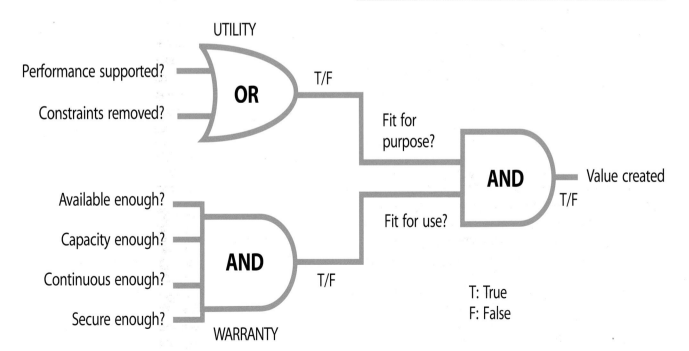

Figure 2.2 Value creation from service utilities and warranties

2.1.4 Service types

Services can be categorized in different types:

- Core services deliver the basic outcomes desired by the customer. They represent the value that the customer wants and for which they are willing to pay
- Supporting services either enable or improve the value of a service. Enabling services are basic factors that enable the provider to serve and enhancing services are excitement factors for differentiation.

2.1.5 Service packaging

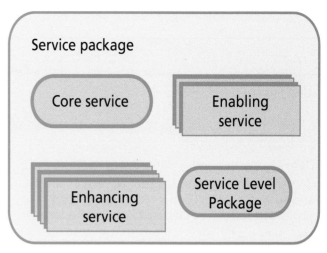

Figure 2.4 Example of a service package

Some supporting services such as Service Desk, typically bundled with most service packages, can also be offered on their own.

> **Definition**
>
> A **service package** is a detailed description of a service that is available to be delivered to customers. A service package includes one or more core services and supporting services, as well as at least one Service Level Package.

Bundling of core services with enabling and enhancing services enables differentiated offerings (Figure 2.3). Services packages come with one or more Service Level Packages (Figure 2.4).

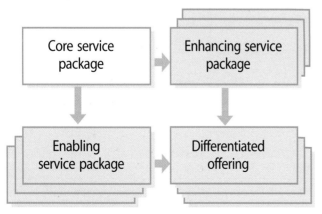

Figure 2.3 Differentiated offerings

Brigitte suddenly realizes that she is part of a very specific customer segment. She is not travelling with her family as a tourist but is recognized by the hotel as a business customer. On the other hand she is probably not considered a VIP by the hotel. The hotel has carefully designed a service package for her segment with room, breakfast, wireless broadband connection, parking and internet booking. It offers different Service Level Packages for her segment as well.

When she booked the hotel, Brigitte had the opportunity to select an ordinary room instead of the suite she chose. The hotel even offered an add-on Service Level Package with the possibility of cancellation until the day of arrival.

2.1.6 Service assets: resources and capabilities

To create value in the form of goods and services, an organization needs service assets. Resources and capabilities are types of service asset.

Brigitte takes a quick walk around the hotel. It's good to be back and it doesn't take her long. Despite its small size, the hotel possesses quite a lot of resources. These include a well-equipped and cosy dining room, a wine cellar, a number of staff members, toilets, information brochures and a car park.

However, Brigitte can't help thinking that the resources would be of no use if it were not for capabilities such as the attitude, skills, knowledge and experience of the staff, their way of organizing the hotel, and a number of well-practised processes that cannot be taken for granted.

Definition

Resource is a generic term, which includes infrastructure, people, money or anything else that might help to deliver a service. Resources are considered to be assets of an organization.

Resources are direct inputs for production.

Capabilities such as management, organization, people and knowledge are used to transform resources into valuable services.

Definition

Capability is the ability of a service organization, person, process, application, Configuration Item or service to carry out an activity. Capabilities are intangible assets of an organization.

The key difference between resource assets and capability assets is that, typically, distinctive capabilities can only be developed over time.

Capabilities reflect experience and are used to transform resources into services; they are firmly embedded within an organization's people, systems, processes and technologies (see Table 2.1).

Table 2.1 Resources and capabilities are types of service asset

Resources	Capabilities
Financial capital	Management
Infrastructure	Organization
Applications	Processes
Information	Knowledge
People	

The distinctive capabilities of a service provider set it apart from its competitors, and enable it to attract and retain customers by offering unique value propositions.

2.1.7 Service composition

A service such as accommodation for one night, which at a first glance looks very simple, seems to be much more complicated behind the scenes. The hotel needs to know Brigitte's 'business process'. Staff need to catalogue their services to help Brigitte select the right service for her needs; they need to sign an agreement with Brigitte, to establish and maintain the appropriate infrastructure at the hotel, to secure and operate the environment, and to gather and maintain data not only about Brigitte but also on all other aspects of the service, such as money, food, facilities and so on.

The hotel needs to provide an internet application, and to acquire supporting services such as wireless access, laundry, newspapers and so on.

The hotel also needs to set up agreements internally with its staff and externally with its suppliers to clarify responsibilities and levels of quality and continually train and measure all parties to ensure a high and consistent quality.

In summary, the composition of a service and its constituent parts can now be defined as illustrated in Figure 2.5.

All the components of the service and their inter-relationships have to be considered, ensuring that the services delivered meet new and evolving business needs. The various components are:

- **Business process** The process that defines the functional needs of the service being provided, e.g. telesales, invoicing, orders, credit checking
- **Service** The service itself that is being delivered to customers and business by the service provider, e.g. e-mail and billing
- **Service Design Package** Document(s) defining all aspects of a service and its requirements through each stage of its lifecycle

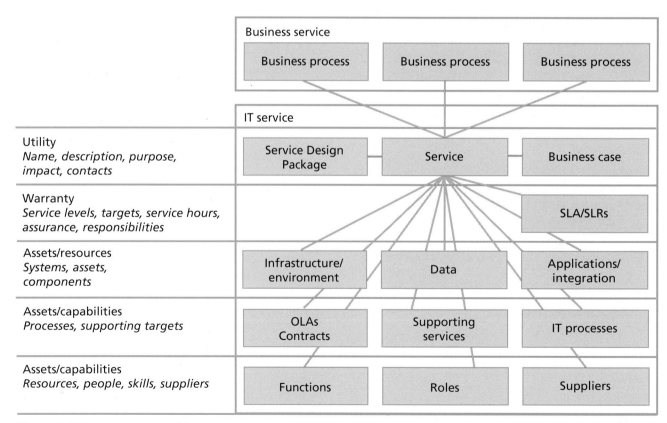

Figure 2.5 Service composition

- **Business case**   Justification for service investments and expenditure
- **Service Level Agreements/Service Level Requirements**   The documents agreed with the customer that specify the level, scope and quality of service to be provided
- **Infrastructure**   All of the IT equipment necessary to deliver the service to customers and users, including servers, network circuits, switches, personal computers (PCs) and telephones
- **Environment**   The environment required to secure and operate the infrastructure, e.g. data centres, power and air conditioning
- **Data**   The data necessary to support the service and provide the information required by the business processes, e.g. customer records and accounts ledger
- **Applications**   All of the software applications required to manipulate the data and provide the functional requirements of the business processes, e.g. Enterprise Resource Management (ERM), Financial and Customer Relationship Management (CRM)
- **Integration**   Solutions to combine applications or data residing at different sources and providing a user or an application with a unified view of these applications and data
- **Operational Level Agreements and contracts**   Any underpinning agreements necessary to deliver the quality of service agreed within a Service Level Agreement (SLA)
- **Supporting services**   Any services that are necessary to support the operation of the delivered service, e.g. a shared service or a managed network service
- **IT processes**   The processes that control and deploy the resources engaged in the service, e.g. Request Fulfilment, Incident Management, Change Management and Availability Management
- **Functions**   Any internal support teams providing second-line and third-line support for any of the components required to provide the service, e.g. the Service Desk
- **Roles**   Responsibilities, activities and authorities granted to a person or team that control and deploy the resources engaged in the service, e.g. Problem Manager, Release Manager, Capacity Manager and Service Owner
- **Suppliers**   Any external third parties necessary to provide third-line and fourth-line support for any of the components required to provide the service.

2.2   PROCESSES, FUNCTIONS AND ROLES

The important capabilities of an organization are its processes, functions and roles.

2.2.1 Processes

Definition

A **process** is a structured set of activities designed to accomplish a specific objective. A process takes one or more defined inputs and turns them into defined outputs.

Brigitte has been at this hotel on a number of occasions, so she recognizes the various processes. The hotel has processes for booking, check-in, cleaning, fulfilling reasonable needs of the guests, managing errors and complaints, ensuring adequate capacity, managing finances, issuing invoices, cooking, dealing with changes or new demands, maintaining buildings and equipment, and check-out.

A process may include any of the roles, responsibilities, tools and management controls required to reliably deliver the outputs.

A process may define policies, standards, guidelines, activities and work instructions if they are needed.

Processes become strategic assets when they create competitive advantage and market differentiation.

2.2.1.1 Closed-loop systems

Process definitions describe actions, dependencies and sequence. Measuring and steering the activities increases effectiveness, and by adding norms to the process, it is possible to add quality measures to the output (Figure 2.6).

Processes are examples of closed-loop systems because they provide change and transformation towards a goal, and use feedback for self-reinforcing and self-corrective action. It is important to consider the entire process or how one process fits into another.

> It occurs to Brigitte that the cleaning of the rooms is a good example. The desired outcome is a clean room. But not everyone agrees to what level 'clean' is. The hotel therefore needs to establish some norms for cleaning and control that the norms are being met. If not, corrective actions must be taken before the process is repeated the next day.

2.2.1.2 Process model

Processes, once defined, should be documented and controlled. Once under control, they can be repeated and become manageable. Degrees of control over processes can be defined, and then process measurement and metrics can be built into the process to control and improve the process, as illustrated in Figure 2.7.

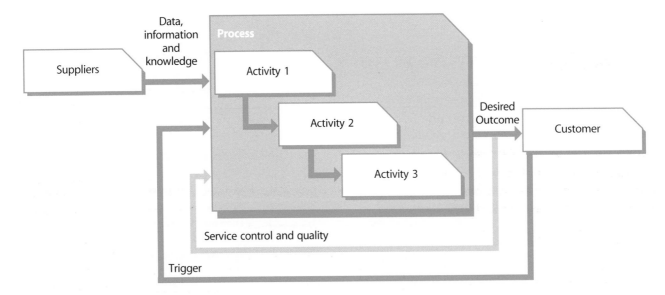

Figure 2.6 A basic process

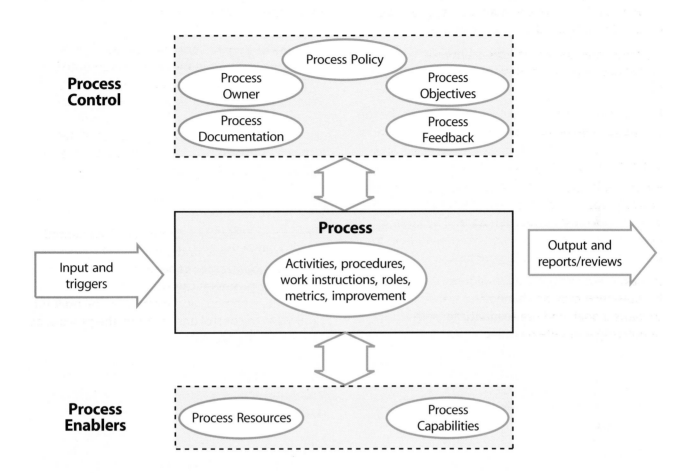

Process Control

Process Policy

Process Owner

Process Objectives

Process Documentation

Process Feedback

Process

Activities, procedures, work instructions, roles, metrics, improvement

Input and triggers

Output and reports/reviews

Process Enablers

Process Resources

Process Capabilities

Figure 2.7 The generic process elements

The generic process elements (Figure 2.7) show that data enters the process, is processed, is output, and the outcome is measured and reviewed.

A process is organized around a set of objectives. The main outputs from the process should be driven by the objectives and should include process measurements (metrics), reports and process improvement.

Each process should be owned by a Process Owner, who should be responsible for the process and its improvement and for ensuring that a process meets its objectives.

The output produced by a process has to conform to operational norms that are derived from business objectives. If products conform to the set norm, the process can be considered effective (because it can be repeated, measured and managed). If the activities are carried out with a minimum use of resources, the process can also be considered efficient. Process analysis, results and metrics should be incorporated in regular management reports and process improvements.

Documentation standards, processes and templates should be used to ensure that the processes are easily adopted throughout an organization.

2.2.1.3 Process characteristics

Processes have the following characteristics. They:

- Are defined in terms of actions, dependencies and sequence
- Are measurable in management terms such as cost and quality, and in practitioner terms such as duration and productivity
- Exist to deliver specific results, which are identifiable and countable
- Have customers or stakeholders with expectations that must be met by the result that the process delivers
- Respond to specific events, which act as triggers for the process.

2.2.2 Functions

> Brigitte sits herself down at the desk in order to go over a few things before the meeting next day, only to realize that the bulb in the lamp on the table has failed. Brigitte calls the reception. It's very easy because the reception acts as a single point of contact to the other functions at the hotel. Soon a staff member from the facilities function knocks on her door and exchanges the bulb.

> **Definition**
>
> A **function** is an organizational unit specialized to perform certain types of work and is responsible for specific outcomes. It is self-contained with capabilities and resources necessary for its performance and outcomes.

In smaller organizations, one person or group can perform multiple functions.

Functions tend to optimize their work methods locally to focus on assigned outcomes. Poor coordination between functions combined with an inward focus leads to functional silos that hinder cross-organizational cooperation.

Well-defined processes can improve productivity within and across functions.

2.2.3 Roles

2.2.3.1 Role

A role refers to a set of connected behaviours or actions that are performed by a person, team or group in a specific context.

> At the small hotel where Brigitte is staying, only a few roles are necessary to manage the delivery of services. In a larger hotel or a hotel chain a greater number of other roles might be needed, such as:
>
> - Account Manager
> - Contract Manager
> - Security Manager
> - Purchasing Manager
> - Project Director
> - Reception Manager.

One person or team may have multiple roles, for example the roles of Configuration Manager and Change Manager may be carried out by a single person.

One person can have more than one role, for example a waiter can work as a dishwasher when the guests have left the restaurant. A small hotel might have just one employee undertaking the two roles, whereas a large hotel is more likely to have only one role per employee.

2.2.3.2 RACI

When designing a service or a process, it is imperative that all the roles are clearly defined. Since processes and their component activities run through an entire organization, the individual activities should be mapped to the roles defined. A RACI authority matrix (see Table 2.2) is often used within organizations to indicate roles and responsibilities in relation to processes and activities. RACI is an acronym for the four main roles of:

- **Responsible** The person or people responsible for getting the job done
- **Accountable** Only one person can be accountable for each activity
- **Consulted** The people who are consulted and whose opinions are sought
- **Informed** The people who are kept up to date on progress.

The example RACI chart (Table 2.2) shows the structure of RACI modelling with the activities down the left-hand side, including the actions that need to be taken and decisions that must be made. Across the top, the chart lists the functional roles responsible for carrying out the initiative or playing a part in decision making.

2.2.4 Process Owner

A Process Owner is accountable for ensuring that their process is being performed according to the agreed and documented process, and that it is meeting the aims of the process definition.

Table 2.2 Example RACI matrix

	Service Manager	Service Level Manager	Problem Manager	Security Manager	Procurement Manager
Activity 1	AR	C	I	I	C
Activity 2	A	R	C	C	C
Activity 3	I	A	R	I	C
Activity 4	I	A	R	I	
Activity 5	I	I	A	C	I

Process Ownership includes such responsibilities as:

- Defining the process strategy
- Defining appropriate policies and standards to be employed throughout the process
- Assisting with and ultimately being responsible for the process design
- Documenting and publicizing the process
- Defining and reviewing the Key Performance Indicators (KPIs) to evaluate the effectiveness and efficiency of the process and taking the required action
- Improving the effectiveness and efficiency of the process
- Communicating process information or changes as appropriate to ensure awareness
- Providing input to the ongoing Service Improvement Plan
- Addressing any issues with the running of the process
- Ensuring all relevant staff have the required training in the process and are aware of their role in the process
- Ensuring that the process, roles, responsibilities and documentation are regularly reviewed and audited
- Interfacing with line management to ensure that the process receives the needed staff resources.

2.2.5 Service Owner

The Service Owner is accountable for a specific service within an organization, regardless of where the underpinning technology components, processes or professional capabilities reside.

Service ownership is as critical to Service Management as establishing ownership for processes, which crosses multiple vertical silos or departments.

The Service Owner:

- Represents the service across the organization
- Understands the service (components etc.)
- Acts as prime customer contact for all service-related enquiries and issues
- Ensures that the ongoing service delivery and support meet agreed customer requirements
- Identifies opportunities for service improvements, discusses these with the customer and raises a Request for Change (RFC) for assessment if appropriate
- Participates in negotiating Service Level Agreements (SLAs) and Operating Level Agreements (OLAs)
- Represents the service in Change Advisory Board (CAB) meetings
- Liaises with the appropriate Process Owners throughout the Service Management lifecycle
- Participates in internal service review meetings within IT and external service review meetings with the business
- Is accountable for the delivery of the service.

2.3 GOOD PRACTICE

Organizations often benchmark themselves against peers and seek to close gaps in capabilities. One way to close such gaps is by adopting good practices.

Practice is a way of working or a way in which work must be done. Practices can include activities, processes, functions, standards and guidelines.

By good or best practice we mean proven activities or processes that have been successfully used by multiple organizations.

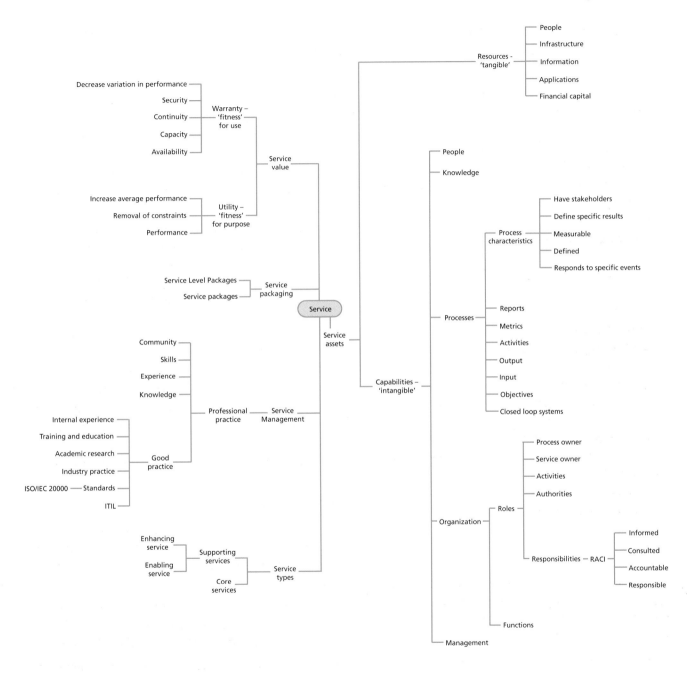

Figure 2.8 Overview of Chapter 2 (Introduction to Service Management)

There are several sources for good practices, including public frameworks, standards and the proprietary knowledge of organizations and individuals:

- ■ Standards
- ■ Industry practices
- ■ Academic research
- ■ Training and education
- ■ Internal experience.

ITIL is an example of good practice. It is used by organizations worldwide to establish and improve capabilities in Service Management.

ISO/IEC 20000 provides a formal and universal standard for organizations seeking to have their Service Management capabilities audited and certified.

2.4 SAMPLE QUESTIONS

1 'Warranty of a service' means:

a The service is fit for purpose.

b There will be no failures in applications and infrastructure associated with the service.

c All service-related problems are fixed free of charge for a certain period of time.

d Customers are assured of certain levels of availability, capacity, continuity and security.

2 Which of the following is the BEST definition of a function?

a It is specialized to perform only one task as a separate entity.

b It is self-contained with capabilities and resources necessary for its performance.

c It is repeatable and becomes manageable.

d It is performance driven and must be able to be measured.

3 A Service Level Manager has been identified with a 'C' in a RACI matrix. Which of the following would be expected of them?

a They are the customer contact.

b They will need to configure their service.

c They will need to be consulted.

d They will need to be communicated to.

4 Which of the following activities is a Process Owner responsible for?

1 Documenting and publicizing the process

2 Participating in negotiating Service Level Agreements

3 Defining Key Performance Indicators (KPIs)

4 Providing input to the ongoing Service Improvement Programme.

a 1 only

b 2 and 3 only

c 1, 3 and 4 only

d All of the above.

5 A Service Owner is accountable for which of the following:

a Carrying out the operational activities to support the service

b Ownership of a service regardless of its underpinning components

c Ownership of a service for all the
   internally managed components of that
   service

d Ensuring that the targets contained
   within a Service Level Agreement are met.

ITIL and the Service Lifecycle

3

3 ITIL and the Service Lifecycle

The Service Lifecycle is iterative and multidimensional. It ensures that organizations are set up to leverage capabilities in one area for learning and for improvements in others.

3.1 THE ITIL SERVICE MANAGEMENT PRACTICES

The objective of the ITIL Service Management practices framework is to provide services to business customers that are fit for purpose, stable and so reliable that the business views them as a trusted utility.

ITIL has been practised successfully around the world for more than 20 years. Over this time, the framework has evolved from a specialized set of Service Management topics with a focus on function, to a process-based framework and now to a broader set of capability-based practices, which provides a holistic Service Lifecycle.

The ITIL Service Management practices framework has the following components:

- **ITIL core guidance** Best-practice guidance applicable to all types of organization that provide services to a business
- **ITIL complementary guidance** A complementary set of publications with guidance specific to industry sectors, organization types, operating models, and technology architectures (this publication is an example of complementary guidance)

- **Web support services** Online, interactive services, which will develop over time and include elements such as the glossary of terms and definitions, the interactive service model, online subscriber services, case studies and templates.

The guidance in ITIL should be adopted and adapted for use in various business environments and organizational strategies.

The complementary guidance provides flexibility to adapt the core practices in a diverse range of environments. Practitioners can select complementary guidance as needed to provide traction for the core in a given business context, much like tyres are selected based on the type of automobile, purpose and road conditions.

3.2 THE SERVICE LIFECYCLE

The structure of the core guidance takes form in a Service Lifecycle. It is iterative and multidimensional. It ensures organizations are set up to leverage capabilities in one area for learning and improvement in others. The Service Lifecycle is described in a set of five core publications (Figure 3.1). Service Design, Service Transition and Service Operation are progressive stages of the lifecycle and represent change and transformation. Service Strategy represents policies and objectives. Continual Service Improvement (CSI) represents learning and improvement.

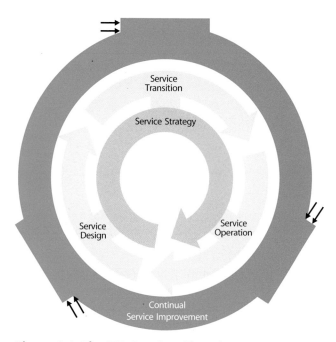

Figure 3.1 The ITIL Service Lifecycle

Service Strategy is the axis around which the lifecycle rotates. Service Design, Service Transition and Service Operation implement strategy. CSI helps place improvement programmes based on strategic objectives.

Each publication addresses capabilities that have a direct impact on a service provider's performance.

3.2.1 Service Strategy

The Service Strategy volume provides guidance on how to design, develop and implement Service Management not only as an organizational capability but also as a strategic asset.

Service Strategy guidance is useful in the context of Service Design, Service Transition, Service Operation and CSI.

Topics covered in Service Strategy include the development of markets, both internal and external, service assets, Service Catalogue and implementation of strategy through the Service Lifecycle. Financial Management, Service Portfolio Management, organizational development and strategic risks are other major topics.

3.2.2 Service Design

The Service Design volume provides guidance for the design and development of services and processes. It covers design principles and methods for converting strategic objectives into portfolios of services and service assets.

The scope of Service Design is not limited to new services. It includes the changes and improvements necessary to increase or maintain value to customers over the lifecycle of services, the continuity of services, achievement of service levels, and conformance to standards and regulations.

3.2.3 Service Transition

The Service Transition volume provides guidance for the development and improvement of capabilities for transitioning new and changed services into operations.

Service Transition provides guidance on how the requirements of Service Strategy encoded in Service Design are effectively realized in Service Operation while controlling the risks of failure and disruption. The publication combines practices in Release Management, programme management and risk management.

3.2.4 Service Operation

The Service Operation volume embodies practices in the management of Service Operation. It includes guidance on achieving effectiveness and efficiency in the delivery and support of services to ensure value for the customer and the service provider.

Strategic objectives are ultimately realized through Service Operations, therefore making it a critical capability. Guidance is provided on ways to maintain stability in Service Operations, allowing for changes in design, scale, scope and Service Levels.

3.2.5 Continual Service Improvement

The Continual Service Improvement (CSI) volume provides instrumental guidance in creating and maintaining value for customers through better design, introduction and operation of services. It combines principles, practices and methods from quality management, Change Management and capability improvement.

Guidance is provided for linking improvement efforts and outcomes with Service Strategy, design and transition.

Last time Brigitte stayed at the hotel, she had a conversation with the hotel manager. He happily told her the history of the hotel. It all began 10 years ago, when a number of industries moved to the area. A local family saw the opportunities for a 'bed-and-breakfast' service, but very soon the need for a hotel arose.

The family used some time to develop their strategy, including identifying the market requirements, defining what services they would deliver, creating a business case, funding, analysing the risks, getting building approval and so on.

When the strategy was clearly defined and the services described, the actual design of the hotel and its services began. This phase involved architects, designers, planners and so on.

After a year the family was ready for transition from the bed-and-breakfast facilities to the new hotel. The hotel was built and inspectors tested that the hotel fulfilled the acceptance criteria and legal regulations, personnel were hired and trained and the hotel opened.

Since then the hotel has been kept operational – through maintenance (plumbers, electricians etc.) and operational services such as garbage collection, cleaning of laundry and a number of other services.

From the very beginning the hotel continually improved its services. Small operational changes have frequently been implemented, training programmes have been improved year after year, and new services such as wireless internet access have been introduced to fulfil the changing requirements of the guests.

Recently the hotel decided to change the Service Strategy to become more than just a hotel; it will house a conference centre in the future. Through the conversation Brigitte realized that it is impossible to talk about the Service Lifecycle. In reality there are many intertwined Service Lifecycles with different extents and cycle frequency.

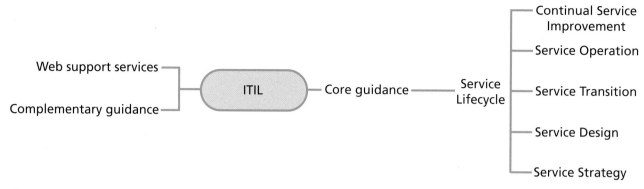

Figure 3.2 Overview of Chapter 3 (ITIL and the Service Lifecycle)

Service Strategy

4   Service Strategy

Service Strategy establishes an overall strategy for services and Service Management – not only as an organizational capability but as a strategic asset.

When the hotel management recently evaluated the strategy of the hotel, including the future portfolio of services, a number of alternatives were analysed:

- Building of a new wing with extra rooms
- Transformation of the hotel into a conference centre
- Expanding of the pool area to a small water world open to the public.

An analysis of the competitive position of the hotel showed that the nearest conference centre was situated about 50 kilometres away. There was a public swimming pool in the town but it had neither a slide nor a jacuzzi.

To support the decision, management needed to identify the option that would provide the highest Return on Investment with the lowest risk. The first move was to prepare a business case on each of the three options.

4.1   GOALS AND OBJECTIVES

It turned out that the most profitable investment was the conference option. The hotel management therefore crafted a plan for transforming the hotel into a conference centre to differentiate the hotel from the other alternatives in the area.

The main goal of Service Strategy is to encourage service providers to think about why something is to be done before thinking of how to do it – that is, to:

- Think and act in a strategic manner
- Operate and grow successfully in the long term
- Transform their Service Management capabilities into a strategic asset
- See and act on the relationships between the services, processes and systems, and the business objectives that they support
- Handle the costs and risks associated with their Service Portfolios.

The main objectives of Service Strategy are to answer questions such as:

- What services should we offer and to whom?
- How do we differentiate ourselves from competing alternatives?
- How do we truly create value for our customers and stakeholders?
- How can we make a case for strategic investments?
- How can Financial Management provide visibility and control over value creation?
- How should we define service quality?
- How do we choose between different paths for improving service quality?
- How do we efficiently allocate resources across a portfolio of services?
- How do we resolve conflicting demands for shared resources?

4.2 SCOPE

The scope of Service Strategy includes:

- Formation and implementation of strategy
- Development of markets and offerings, internal and external
- Service assets and value creation
- Service Portfolio Management and Service Catalogue
- Financial Management
- Demand Management
- Organizational development and culture
- Sourcing strategy
- Strategic risks.

4.3 VALUE CREATION

4.3.1 Value

Brigitte's eye catches the information pamphlet that the hotel has left on the table in her room. It contains a number of services such as a wake-up call, parking, laundry service, dining and childcare as well as descriptive attributes of the services such as the number of television channels, cleaning of the room and breakfast times.

Brigitte finds most of the services valuable, even though she doesn't need the childcare service on this occasion. But to Brigitte the described services are only a part of what she appreciates as a hotel guest. For her it is as important that the hotel is situated close to her temporary workplace, that the staff are kind and obliging, that her balcony has a beautiful view over the Alps and that the hotel respects her preference for vegetarian food.

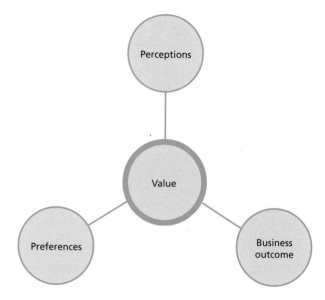

Figure 4.1 Value as a function of preferences, perceptions and business outcome

Customers do not buy services. They buy the fulfilment of particular needs. What counts is quality as it is perceived by customers. The value of a service is therefore determined by what the customer prefers (preferences), what the customer perceives (perceptions) and what the customer actually gets (business outcome) (Figure 4.1).

Consequently service providers have to demonstrate business outcomes, influence perceptions and respond to preferences.

Customers have reference values on which they base their perceptions of a service. The economic value of the service can be defined as the sum of this reference value, the utility (increase in possible gains from the service) and the warranty (decrease in possible losses for the customer) of the service.

What the customer values is frequently different from what the IT organization believes it provides. Mind the gap!

What are the outcomes that matter? How are they identified and ranked in terms of customer perceptions and preferences? Effectiveness in answering such questions requires a marketing mindset. A marketing mindset begins with simple questions that can only be answered by the customers:

- What is our business?
- Who is our customer?
- What does the customer value?
- Who depends on our services?
- How do they use our services?
- Why are they valuable to them?

4.3.2 Value creation

Resources and capabilities are types of asset. Organizations use them to create value in the form of goods and services.

Capabilities are developed over time. The development of capabilities is enhanced by the experience gained from the number and variety of customers, market spaces, contracts and services. Experience is similarly enriched from solving problems, handling situations, managing risks and analysing failures.

Capabilities by themselves cannot produce value without resources. The productive capacity of a service provider is dependent on the resources under their control. Capabilities are used to develop, deploy and coordinate this productive capacity.

4.4 KEY PRINCIPLES

4.4.1 Service Portfolio

The delivery of the hotel services requires comprehensive knowledge about customers, contracts, services and supporting assets such as furniture and equipment, staff members, suppliers and processes. To manage this knowledge, the hotel established a number of supporting systems some years ago, including:

- A registry of services and their interdependencies
- A customer catalogue presenting the services provided by the hotel
- Service Level Agreements with travel agencies and larger companies
- A configuration database containing data for all relevant equipment, people, suppliers and processes that underpin the provided services.

The registry of services has since supported the management in deciding which services to offer or invest in, e.g. overnight stay, dining or conference services. The registry contains all the services provided to the customers, suggestions for new or changed services as well as supporting services such as laundry cleaning, internet access, pool cleaning and garbage collection.

The customer catalogue is aimed at the customers and guests. When Brigitte planned her trip to Switzerland she looked up the hotel on the internet. On the hotel's homepage she found information on the services provided:

- Overnight stay

- Single guest room, €100 per night
- Double guest room, €150 per night
- Suite (with table and free internet connection), €170 per night
- Executive room (with separate bedroom and living room, €200 per night

■ Dinner at the restaurant
  - Two courses (€30 per person)
  - Three courses (€40 per person)

■ Swimming pool (€5 per hour – free for guests at the hotel).

As Brigitte was pleased with the hotel services (especially the restaurant and swimming pool), she ordered a suite.

The Service Portfolio is the most critical management system used to support all processes. It describes a provider's services in terms of business value, the business needs addressed and how the service provider responds to those needs.

The Portfolio Management approach helps managers prioritize investments and improve the allocation of resources. Changes to portfolios are governed by policies and procedures.

Definition

The **Service Portfolio** is the complete set of services that are managed by a service provider.

The Service Portfolio represents all the resources presently engaged or being released in various stages of the Service Lifecycle.

The Service Portfolio is used to manage the entire lifecycle of all services, and includes three categories:

■ Service Pipeline (proposed or in development)

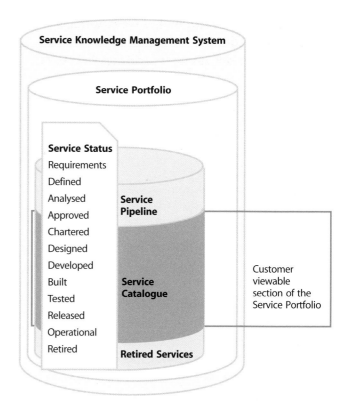

Figure 4.2 The Service Portfolio and its contents

■ Service Catalogue (live or available for deployment)
■ Retired services.

The portfolio also includes third-party services, which are an integral part of service offerings to customers. Some third-party services are visible to the customers whereas others are not.

By acting as the basis of a decision framework, a Service Portfolio either clarifies or helps to clarify the following strategic questions:

■ Why should a customer buy these services?
■ Why should they buy these services from us?
■ What are the pricing or chargeback models?

- What are our strengths and weaknesses, priorities and risks?
- How should our resources and capabilities be allocated?

The registry of services was supposed to support the management of the hotel in answering questions such as:

- What value does an overnight stay at our hotel provide to the guests compared with similar rival hotels?
- Which supporting services, resources and capabilities are needed to provide the conference service?
- What risks are associated with dining services?

As the registry became more and more complete and reliable over time, it also became more and more critical as a means to support the hotel management in making the right decisions on the optimal use of the available resources and capabilities.

Brigitte can't stop thinking about the practice of the hotel maintaining a registry of all its services, not only the services that are provided to the guests, but also the underpinning services such as cleaning and cooking.

She realizes that the hotel needs not only to maintain the registry of the guest services and the supporting services, but also to identify and maintain the relationships between the services. To provide an overnight stay, the hotel needs to provide cleaning and (if the guest requests it) wireless internet as well.

Service Portfolio	Service Catalogue(s)
Description	Services
Value proposition	Supported products
Business cases	Policies
Priorities	Ordering and request procedures
Risks	Support terms and conditions
Offerings and packages	Entry points and escalations
Cost and pricing	Pricing and chargeback

Figure 4.3 Elements of a Service Portfolio and Service Catalogue

4.4.2 Service Catalogue

Customers and users would only be allowed access to those services within the Service Portfolio that were of a status between 'chartered' and 'operational', as illustrated by the box in Figure 4.2, namely those services contained within the Service Catalogue. The Service Catalogue is the only part of the Service Portfolio visible to current or prospective customers, and it is used to support the sale and delivery of services.

The Service Catalogue is also the only part of the Portfolio that recovers costs or earns profits.

Definition

A **Service Catalogue** is a database or structured document with information about all live services, including those available for deployment and operation.

The Service Catalogue includes information about deliverables, prices, contact points, ordering and request processes (Figure 4.3).

It is in the Service Catalogue that services are decomposed into components; it is where assets, processes and systems are introduced with entry points and terms for their use and provisioning. As providers may have many customers or serve many businesses, there may be multiple Service Catalogues chartered from the Service Portfolio.

4.4.3 Business case

A service provider will need to make decisions on what Service Management initiatives it wishes to invest in. The business case for these investments is key to this decision-making process.

A business case is a decision-support and planning tool. It describes the objectives and the likely outcomes of a business decision. The outcomes can take on qualitative and quantitative dimensions.

> **Definition**
>
> A **business case** is a justification for a significant item of expenditure. It includes information about costs, benefits, options, issues, risks and possible problems.

The business case articulates the objectives of the initiative and the specific business impacts (costs, risks and benefits) that the initiative is expected to generate (see Table 4.1).

The financial consequence of a decision, typically in the form of Return on Investment (ROI), is often a core component of a business case.

Table 4.1 Sample business case structure

Business case structure
A. Introduction Presents the business objectives addressed by the service
B. Methods and assumptions Defines the boundaries of the business case, such as time period, whose costs and whose benefits
C. Business impacts The financial and non-financial business case results
D. Risks and contingencies The probability that alternative results will emerge
E. Recommendations Specific actions recommended

A well-rounded business case also covers an analysis of the desired non-financial business impacts associated with the initiative, forming clear linkages between these non-financial impacts and a recognized business objective. This analysis may use the Value on Investment (VOI) technique.

4.4.4 Management of risk

Risk analysis and risk management should be applied to the Service Pipeline and Service Catalogue to identify and mitigate risks within the Service Lifecycle.

4.4.4.1 Risk

> **Definition**
>
> **Risk** is a possible event that could cause harm or loss, or affect the ability to achieve objectives.

A risk is measured by the probability of a threat, the vulnerability of the asset to that threat, and the impact if it occurred (Figure 4.4).

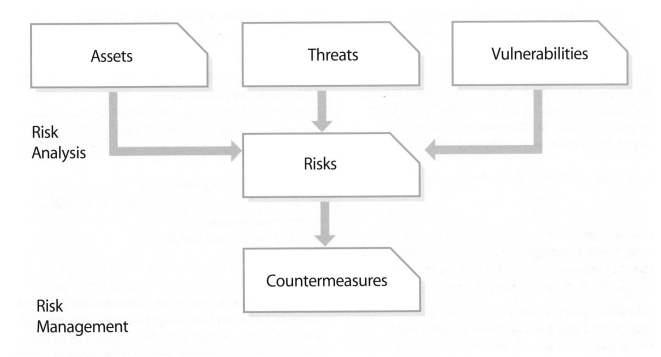

Figure 4.4 Risk, risk analysis and risk management

4.4.4.2 Risk analysis

Risk analysis is concerned with gathering information about exposure to risk so that the organization carrying out the risk analysis can make appropriate decisions and manage risk appropriately. Risk analysis involves the identification and assessment of the level of the risks calculated from the assessed values of assets and the assessed levels of threats to, and vulnerabilities of, those assets.

4.4.4.3 Risk management

Risk management involves having processes in place to monitor risks, access to reliable and up-to-date information about risks, the right balance of control in place to deal with those risks,

and decision-making processes supported by a framework of risk analysis and evaluation.

Risk management also involves the identification, selection and adoption of countermeasures justified by the identified risks.

4.5 PROCESSES

The ITIL Foundation syllabus covers the following Service Strategy processes:

- Demand Management
- Financial Management.

In addition the Service Strategy book includes the Strategy Generation and Service Portfolio Management processes, but as these are not part of the ITIL Foundation syllabus they will not be further discussed.

4.5.1 Demand Management

Brigitte takes a closer look on the flyer next to the telephone. She notices that the hotel offers a special family discount in August. She can't avoid wondering why the hotel reduces its prices during the holiday season, a time when the hotel should appeal to tourists in the area.

Next time she passes the reception she decides to ask the receptionist why the hotel offers a family discount in August. No sooner said than done. He answers that very few tourists have chosen to stay at the hotel in August the last two years. The hotel management therefore discussed the situation based on that pattern and identified three possible solutions:

1 Lowering the prices for families to attract tourists

2 Introducing new services to attract tourists (e.g. expand the pool area to a small water world)

3 Closing the hotel for one month.

4.5.1.1 Goals and objectives

- To avoid excess capacity-generating costs without creating value
- To prevent insufficient capacity that impacts on the quality of services delivered.

4.5.1.2 Basic concepts

Services cannot be produced in advance of when they are consumed. Therefore it is essential that the service provider achieves a tight synchronization of supply capacity and service demand.

Activity-based Demand Management

Business processes are the primary source of demand for services.

It is therefore very important to study the customer's business to identify, analyse and codify the Patterns of Business Activity to provide sufficient basis for Capacity Management. Analysing and tracking the activity patterns of the business process makes it possible to predict demand for services. It is also possible to predict demand for underlying service assets that support those services.

Patterns of Business Activity

Customer assets such as people, processes and applications generate Patterns of Business Activity.

Definition

Pattern of Business Activity (PBA) is a workload profile of one or more business activities. Patterns of Business Activity are used to help the service provider understand and plan for different levels of business activity.

Demand Management therefore includes identification, analysis, codification and visualization of the customer's business activity and plans in terms of the demand for supporting services.

One or more attributes such as frequency, volume, location and duration describe business activity. They are associated with requirements such as security, privacy and latency or tolerance for delays. This profile of business activity can alter over time with changes and improvements in business processes, people, organization, applications and infrastructure.

User profiles

> **Definition**
>
> A **user profile** (UP) is a pattern of user demand for services. Each user profile includes one or more Patterns of Business Activity.

User profiles are based on roles and responsibilities within organizations for people, and functions and operations for processes and applications. User profiles are constructed using one or more predefined Patterns of Business Activity. They are also under change control. User profiles represent patterns that are persistent and correlated.

Pattern matching using Patterns of Business Activity and user profiles ensures a systematic approach to understanding and managing demand from customers.

4.5.1.3 Challenges

Demand Management is a critical aspect of Service Management. Poorly managed demand is a source of risk for service providers because of uncertainty in demand. Typical challenges faced by Demand Management include:

- Excess capacity generating cost without creating value that provides a basis for cost recovery. Customers are reluctant to pay for idle capacity unless it has value for them
- Insufficient capacity having an impact on the quality of services delivered and limiting the growth of the service
- Synchronous production and consumption. Unlike goods, services cannot be manufactured in advance and stockpiled in a finished goods inventory in anticipation of demand.

4.5.2 Financial Management

Next door to the hotel a new restaurant opened a couple of months ago. As a consequence the hotel restaurant has more than halved its number of guests. The staff level in the restaurant has been adapted accordingly. At the weekly management team meeting the situation is being discussed. It is a very emotional discussion – should the restaurant be closed or not? The Financial Manager is asked to prepare a financial assessment of the restaurant.

At the next meeting the Financial Manager presents his analysis: the restaurant is only just profitable. But the hotel management decides to keep it, as it provides a more seamless service provision to the guests if the hotel runs its own restaurant. Further, the hotel is expected to expand during the coming years: more rooms are expected to be added and a conference centre will generate more customers for the restaurant.

4.5.2.1 Goals and objectives

- To provide operational visibility, insight and superior decision making
- To provide the business and IT with the quantification, in financial terms, of the value of IT services, the value of the assets underlying the provisioning of those services, and the qualification of operational forecasting
- To ensure proper funding for the delivery and consumption of services.

4.5.2.2 Basic concepts

Talking about IT in terms of services is the heart of changing the perception of IT and its value to the business. Therefore, a significant portion of Financial Management is working in tandem with IT and the business to help identify, document and agree on the value of the services being received, and the enablement of service demand modelling and management.

Service Valuation

Service Valuation is used within Financial Management to identify:

- **Provisioning value**   The cost to the service provider of delivering a specific service to a customer. This includes costs associated with hardware and software, annual maintenance fees, personnel, facilities and power consumption, compliance, taxes and interest charges
- **Service value potential**   Techniques such as service-oriented accounting used to associate specific monetary values with each perceived value-added component of the service. The sum of the perceived values is the service value potential, which is added to the provisioning value to calculate the ultimate value of the service.

Demand modelling

Financial demand modelling focuses on identifying the total cost of utilization to the customer and predicting the financial implications of future service demand.

Service Provisioning Optimization

Financial Management provides key inputs for Service Provisioning Optimization (SPO). SPO examines the financial inputs and constraints of service components or delivery models to determine whether alternatives should be explored relating to how a service can be provisioned differently to make it more competitive in terms of cost or quality.

Planning and budgeting

Planning provides financial translation and qualification of expected future demand for services.

Service Investment Analysis

The objective of Service Investment Analysis is to derive a value indication for the total lifecycle of a service based on the value received and costs incurred during the lifecycle of the service.

Accounting

The functions and accounting characteristics are typically:

- **Service recording**   The assignment of a cost entry to the appropriate service
- **Cost types**   Higher-level expense categories such as hardware, software, resource and administration
- **Cost classifications**   Classifications within services that designate the end purpose of the cost. These include classifications such as:
  - Capital/operational
  - Direct/indirect
  - Fixed/variable
  - Cost units.

Compliance

Compliance relates to the ability to demonstrate that proper and consistent accounting methods and/or practices are being employed.

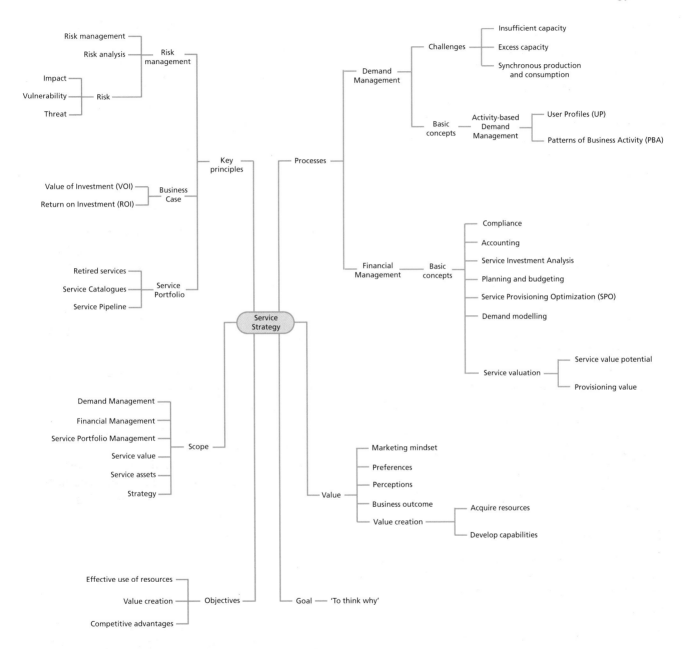

Figure 4.5 Overview of Chapter 4 (Service Strategy)

4.6 SAMPLE QUESTIONS

1 What is NOT an output from Service Strategy:

 a The Service Design Package

 b Policies and objectives

 c Agreements on resource allocation

 d The Service Portfolio.

2 How is the value of a service determined?

 a By whether the service performs to its performance commitments

 b By whether the appropriate services are contained in the Service Catalogue

 c By whether the customer perceives their preferences have met the desired business outcome

 d By whether the service has been designed in accordance with the business case.

3 The Service Portfolio is a critical management system. What does it contain?

 a Details of all live operational services

 b A full list of business projects and when they are due for implementation

 c Details of all third-party services

 d The complete set of services that are managed by the service provider.

4 A business case should contain:

 1 Business impacts

 2 Risks and contingencies

 3 Costs and benefits

 4 A solution specification.

 a 1, 2 and 4 only

 b 3 and 4 only

 c 1, 2 and 3 only

 d All of the above.

Service Design

5   Service Design

The Service Design stage takes business requirements and creates services, their supporting practices and management tools which meet business demands for quality, reliability and flexibility.

Later that afternoon Brigitte notices an assembly of a group of local people in the hotel lobby. She can't help being curious and asks the first one she meets what is going on. It turns out that the hotel has arranged a meeting for the businesses in the area to uncover their needs for local conference services and facilities.

Later the hotel manager explains that a local architect has been selected to design the facilities based on input from the meeting as well as requirements collected through a survey performed among the guests in past months.

But he also stresses that the conference building and facilities are probably the smallest challenges when designing the new conference service. A project manager has therefore temporarily been hired to redesign processes, hire people, assign responsibilities, develop sales material and so on.

5.1   GOALS AND OBJECTIVES

The main goal is the design of a new or changed service for introduction into the live environment.

The main objectives of Service Design are to:

- Design services to satisfy business objectives that can easily and efficiently be maintained and enhanced
- Design processes for the design, transition, operation and improvement of IT services
- Identify and manage risks so that they can be removed or mitigated
- Design secure and resilient technologies, resources and capability
- Design measurement methods and metrics for assessing the process effectiveness and efficiency
- Produce and maintain IT plans, processes, policies, standards, architectures, frameworks and documents for the design of quality IT solutions
- Develop the IT skills and capability within.

5.2   SCOPE

There are five aspects in the scope of Service Design, covering the design of:

1   New or changed services

2   The Service Management systems and tools, including the Service Portfolio and Service Catalogues

3   The technology architecture and management systems

4   The processes, roles, responsibilities and skills required

5   Measurement methods and metrics.

Service Design starts with a set of business requirements and ends with the development of a service solution designed to meet the documented needs of the business.

This developed solution design, together with its Service Design Package, is then passed to Service Transition to evaluate, build, test and deploy the new or changed service. On completion of these transition activities, control is transferred to the Service Operation stage of the Service Lifecycle.

5.3 BUSINESS VALUE

With good Service Design it will be possible to deliver quality and cost-effective services, and ensure that the business requirements are being met.

The following benefits are examples of results of good Service Design practice:

- **Reduced total cost of ownership** Cost of ownership can be minimized if all aspects of services, processes and technology are designed properly and implemented against the design
- **Improved quality and consistency of service** Both service and operational quality will be enhanced and services will be designed within the corporate strategy, architectures and constraints
- **More effective Service Management and processes** Processes will be designed with optimal quality and cost-effectiveness
- **Improved service alignment** Involvement from the conception of the service ensures that new or changed services match business needs, with services designed to meet Service Level Requirements.

5.4 KEY PRINCIPLES

5.4.1 The five major aspects of design

An overall, integrated approach should be adopted for the design activities, covering the design of:

1 The service solutions, including all of the functional requirements, resources and capabilities needed and agreed

2 Service Management systems and tools, especially the Service Portfolio for the management of services through their lifecycle

3 Technology architectures and management systems and tools required to provide the services

4 The processes, roles and responsibilities needed to design, transition, operate and improve the services

5 The measurement methods and metrics for the services, architectures and their constituent components, and the processes.

The main reason for the hotel manager to engage an interim project manager was to ensure a holistic approach to the design of the conference services. The project manager has therefore been made responsible for ensuring that all design aspects of the services are considered, including:

- Design of the new conference facilities (buildings, access, parking, staff requirements etc.)
- Design of the overall monitoring needed, e.g. the heating, the elevator and the fire alarm

- Design of the architecture, e.g. the hotel has to look homogeneous, fit into the environment and still be easy to maintain
- Redesign of relevant processes, such as the booking process to include meeting rooms and equipment
- Design of metrics and measurement systems for measurement of meeting room occupancy rates, customer satisfaction etc.

5.4.1.1 Service solution

The key aspect is the design of new or changed service solutions to meet changing business needs. The tasks to be carried out include:

- Analyse the business requirements
- Explore opportunities for re-use
- Produce service solution design
- Create and maintain the Service Acceptance Criteria (SAC)
- Evaluate and cost alternative designs
- Agree the expenditure and budgets
- Re-evaluate and confirm the business benefits
- Agree the preferred solution and its Service Level Requirements (SLRs)
- Ensure the solution is in line with strategies, policies and architecture, and make proposals for change if not
- Ensure corporate and IT governance and security controls are taken into account
- Complete an organizational readiness assessment
- Identify requirements for suppliers and supporting contracts.

A Service Design Package should be assembled during the design stage for each new service, major change or service retirement to document the service solution.

> **Definition**
>
> A **Service Design Package** is a document defining all aspects of a service and its requirements through each stage of its lifecycle.

The Service Design Package must contain everything necessary for the subsequent testing, introduction and operation of the solution or service.

This package is then passed from Service Design to Service Transition and details all aspects of the service and its requirements through all of the subsequent stages of its lifecycle.

Figure 5.1 shows the lifecycle of a service from the initial or changed business requirement through the design, transition and operation stages of the lifecycle.

5.4.1.2 Service Management systems and tools

The Service Management systems and tools, especially the Service Portfolio, should be considered to ensure that a new or changed service is consistent with all other services, and that all other services that interface, support or depend on the new or changed services are consistent with the new service. If not, either the design of the new service or the other existing services will need to be adapted.

Also the Service Management systems and tools should be reviewed to ensure they are capable of supporting the new or changed service.

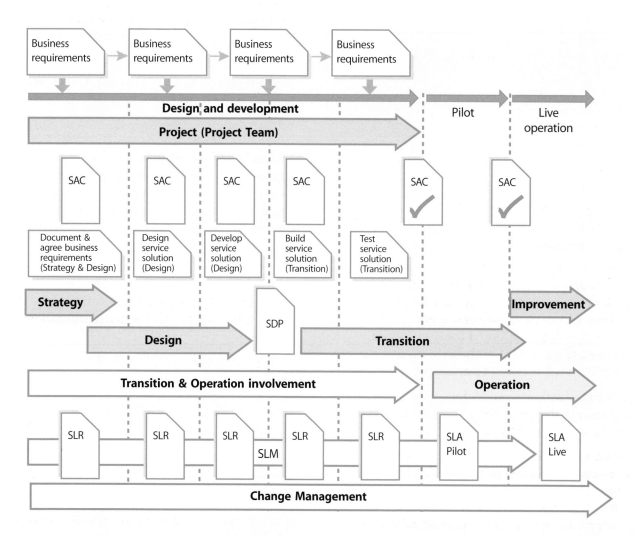

Figure 5.1 Aligning new services to business requirements

5.4.1.3 Architecture and management systems

The technology architectures and management systems should be considered to ensure that all the technology architectures and management systems are consistent with a new or changed service and have the capability to operate and maintain the new service. If not, then either the architectures or management systems will need to be amended or the design of the new service will need to be revised.

5.4.1.4 Processes

All IT and Service Management processes need to be considered to ensure that the processes, roles, responsibilities and skills have the capability to operate, support and maintain a new or changed service. If not, the design of the new service will need to be revised or the existing process capabilities will need to be enhanced.

Each organization should adopt a formalized approach to the design and implementation of Service Management processes.

The objective should not be to design 'perfect processes', but to design practical and appropriate processes with 'in-built' improvement mechanisms, so that the effectiveness and efficiency of the processes are improved in the most suitable manner for an organization.

Documentation standards, processes and templates should be used to ensure that the processes are easily adopted throughout the organization.

5.4.1.5 Measurement methods and metrics

The measurement methods and metrics should be considered to ensure that the existing measurement methods can provide the required metrics on a new or changed service. If not, then the measurement methods will need to be enhanced or the service metrics will need to be revised.

There are four types of metrics that can be used to measure the capability and performance of processes:

- **Progress** Milestones and deliverables in the capability of the process
- **Compliance** Compliance of the process with governance requirements, regulatory requirements and compliance of people to the process
- **Effectiveness** The accuracy and correctness of the process and its ability to deliver the 'right result'
- **Efficiency** The productivity of the process, its speed, throughput and resource utilization.

5.4.2 People, processes, products and partners – the four Ps

Looking out of the window, Brigitte notices a service technician entering the hotel from the back entrance. On the car it says 'Electrician – call Jacob at (4) 270435'. Brigitte wonders whether Jacob is a regular supplier to the hotel or just an electrician called in to solve a specific issue.

She realizes that management has to decide whether they want to hire people (employees) to get a job done or to contract with partners like Jacob.

Irrespective of whether they hire their own people or use external partners, management has to decide how the business should be run and describe the related processes.

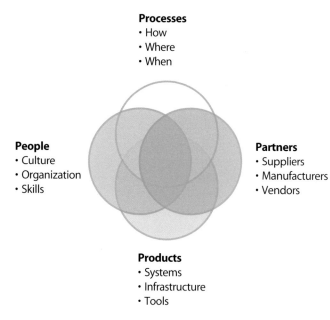

Processes
• How
• Where
• When

People
• Culture
• Organization
• Skills

Partners
• Suppliers
• Manufacturers
• Vendors

Products
• Systems
• Infrastructure
• Tools

Figure 5.2 The four Ps

Good Service Design is dependent on effective and efficient use of the 'four Ps' (Figure 5.2): people, processes, products and partners.

When designing a new or changed service, Service Design focuses on ensuring that the 'four Ps' are taken into account at every stage throughout the Service Lifecycle. This is achieved through the five major design aspects described in section 5.4.1.

5.5 PROCESSES

The ITIL Foundation syllabus covers the following Service Design processes:

■ Service Catalogue Management
■ Service Level Management
■ Supplier Management
■ Capacity Management
■ Availability Management

■ Service Continuity Management
■ Information Security Management.

5.5.1 Service Catalogue Management

5.5.1.1 Goals and objectives

■ To provide a single source of consistent information on all of the agreed services and ensure that it is widely available to those who are approved to access it
■ To ensure that a Service Catalogue is produced and maintained and is accurate and current.

5.5.1.2 Basic concepts

Service Catalogues

The Service Catalogue has two aspects (Figure 5.3):

■ The Business Service Catalogue, containing details of all of the services delivered to the customer, together with relationships to the business units and processes that rely on the services. This is the customer view
■ The Technical Service Catalogue, containing details of all of the services delivered to the customer, together with relationships to the supporting or shared services and Configuration Items (CIs) necessary to support the provision of the service to the business. This should underpin the Business Service Catalogue and not form part of the customer view.

Some organizations only maintain either a Business Service Catalogue or a Technical Service Catalogue. The preferred situation adopted by the more mature organizations maintains both aspects within a single Service Catalogue, which is part of a totally integrated Service Management activity and Service Portfolio.

Service Catalogue

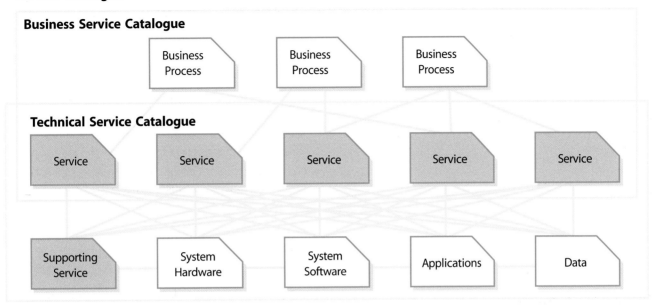

Business Service Catalogue

Business Process

Business Process

Business Process

Technical Service Catalogue

Service

Service

Service

Service

Service

Supporting Service

System Hardware

System Software

Applications

Data

Figure 5.3 The Business Service Catalogue and the Technical Service Catalogue

5.5.2 Service Level Management

Last time Brigitte checked out of the hotel the receptionist had asked: 'Did your stay meet your expectations?'

Brigitte realized that she had not been aware of what she actually expected from the stay. She had ordered a suite for one night. Of course she had expected the room to be clean, to smell good, and the bed neither to be too soft nor too hard. She had furthermore expected hot milk for her morning coffee and fresh fruit as well as cheese and bread for breakfast. From the hotel homepage she had got the feeling that the staff had a warm and friendly attitude towards guests. Fortunately most of her expectations were met – except for the hot milk.

'Yes, my stay did live up to my expectations.' Brigitte noticed that the receptionist typed her answer into the IT system.

Brigitte may have looked puzzled, because the receptionist had continued: 'We normally don't sign agreements with our guests documenting mutual expectations. But we often do it with the travel agencies. I am currently negotiating an agreement with a travel agency, where we discuss service levels such as restaurant opening hours and room service.'

5.5.2.1 Goals and objectives

■ To ensure that an agreed level of service is provided for all services and that the services and their performance are measured in a consistent way

- To define, document, agree, monitor, measure, report and review the level of services provided
- To provide and improve the relationship and communication with the business and customers
- To ensure that proactive measures to improve the levels of service delivered are implemented wherever it is cost-justifiable to do so.

5.5.2.2 Basic concepts

Service provider and supplier

> **Definition**
>
> A **service provider** is an organization supplying services to one or more internal customers or external customers.

It is necessary to distinguish between different types of service provider. There are three archetypes of service provider:

- **Type I** Internal service provider: exists within an organization solely to deliver service to one specific business unit
- **Type II** Shared services unit: services multiple business units in the same organization
- **Type III** External service provider: operates from outside the organization, servicing multiple customers.

> **Definition**
>
> A **supplier** is a third party responsible for supplying goods or services that are required to deliver services.

Examples of suppliers include commodity hardware and software vendors, network and telecom providers, and outsourcing organizations.

Service Level Agreement

Service Level Agreements provide the basis for managing the relationship between the service provider and the customer.

> **Definition**
>
> A **Service Level Agreement** (SLA) is an agreement between a service provider and the customer(s). The SLA describes the service, service level targets and the responsibilities of the service provider and the customer. A single SLA may cover multiple services or multiple customers.

Service Level Requirement

Service Level Agreements are based on requirements from the customers. It is advisable to involve customers from the outset, but rather than going along with a blank sheet to start with, it may be better to produce a first outline draft of the performance targets and the management and operational requirements, as a starting point for more detailed and in-depth discussion.

> **Definition**
>
> A **Service Level Requirement** (SLR) is a customer requirement for an aspect of a service. SLRs are based on business objectives and are used to negotiate agreed service level targets.

The SLRs should be an integral part of the Service Design criteria, of which the functional specification is a part. They should, from the very start, form part of the testing criteria as the service progresses through the stages of design and development or procurement.

This SLR will gradually be refined as the service progresses through the stages of its lifecycle, until it eventually becomes a pilot SLA during the early life support period.

SLA framework

Using the Service Catalogue as an aid, Service Level Management must design the most appropriate SLA structure to ensure that all services and all customers are covered in a manner best suited to the organization's needs. There are a number of potential options, including the following.

Service-based SLA

This is where an SLA covers one service, for all the customers of that service – for example, an SLA may be established for an organization's e-mail service, covering all the customers of that service.

Customer-based SLA

This is an agreement with an individual customer group, covering all the services they use. For example, agreements may be reached with an organization's finance department covering, say, the finance system, the accounting system, the payroll system, the billing system, the procurement system and any other IT systems that they use. Customers often prefer such an agreement, as all of their requirements are covered in a single document. Only one signatory is normally required, which simplifies this issue.

Multi-level SLAs

Some organizations have chosen to adopt a multi-level SLA structure. For example, a three-layer structure as follows:

- **Corporate level** Covering all the generic SLM issues appropriate to every customer throughout the organization; these issues are likely to be less volatile, so updates are less frequently required

- **Customer level** Covering all SLM issues relevant to the particular customer group or business unit, regardless of the service being used

- **Service level** Covering all SLM issues relevant to the specific service, in relation to a specific customer group (one for each service covered by the SLA).

Operational Level Agreements and Underpinning Contracts

The SLAs are underpinned by Operational Level Agreements (OLAs) and Underpinning Contracts (Figure 5.4).

> **Definition**
>
> An **Operational Level Agreement** (OLA) is an underpinning agreement between a service provider and another part of the same organization that assists with the provision of services. The OLA defines the goods or services to be provided and the responsibilities of both parties.

For example, there could be an OLA between:

- The service provider and a procurement department to obtain hardware at agreed times
- The Service Desk and a support group to provide incident resolution within agreed times.

> **Definition**
>
> An **Underpinning Contract** (UC) is a legally binding agreement between a service provider and a third party, called the supplier. The Underpinning Contract defines targets and responsibilities that are required to meet agreed service level targets in an SLA.

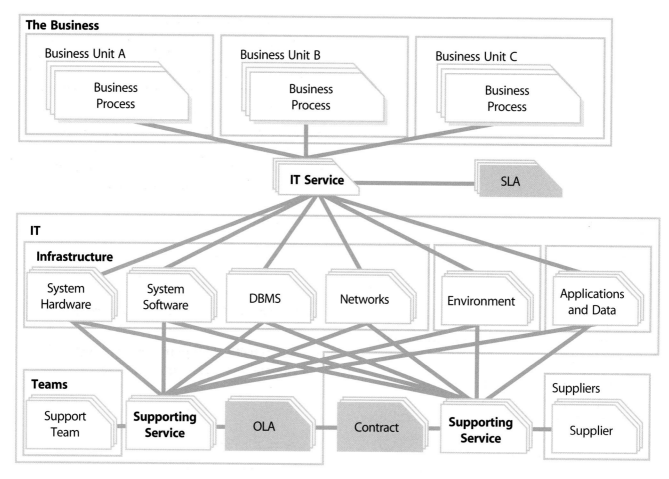

Figure 5.4 Service Level Agreements (SLAs), Operational Level Agreements (OLAs) and Underpinning Contracts

Service reports

Periodic service level reports must be produced and circulated to customers and appropriate IT managers. The periodic reports should incorporate details of performance against all SLA targets, together with details of any trends or specific actions being undertaken to improve service quality.

A useful technique is to include an SLA Monitoring (SLAM) chart at the front of a service report to give an 'at-a-glance' overview of how achievements have measured up against targets.

Definition

A **Service Level Agreement Monitoring** (SLAM) chart is used to help monitor and report achievements against service level targets. SLAM charts are typically colour coded (red, amber and green, and sometimes referred to as RAG charts as a result) to show whether each agreed service level target has been met, missed or nearly missed during each of the previous 12 months.

Service Improvement Plans and Service Reviews

Periodic review meetings must be held regularly with customers (or their representatives) to review the service achievement in the last period and to preview any issues for the coming period. It is normal to hold such meetings monthly or, as a minimum, quarterly.

Actions must be placed on the customer and provider as appropriate to improve weak areas where targets are not being met. All actions must be minuted, and progress should be reviewed at the next meeting to ensure that action items are being followed up and properly implemented.

This is valuable input to the Service Improvement Plans (SIPs) for the management, planning and implementation of all service and process improvements.

Definition

A **Service Improvement Plan** (SIP) is a formal plan to implement improvements to a process or service.

All agreements and underpinning agreements, including SLAs, Underpinning Contracts and OLAs, must be kept up to date. They should be reviewed periodically, at least annually, to ensure that they are still current and comprehensive, and are still aligned to business needs and strategy.

These reviews should ensure that the services covered and the targets for each are still relevant – and that nothing significant has changed that invalidates the agreement in any way.

5.5.2.3 Process activities

Service Level Management includes the process of planning, coordinating, drafting, agreeing, monitoring and reporting of SLAs and the ongoing review of service achievements to ensure that the required and cost-justifiable service quality is maintained and gradually improved.

The key activities within the Service Level Management process (Figure 5.5) are:

- Design SLA frameworks, including making available and maintaining up-to-date Service Level Management document templates and standards
- Determine, negotiate, document and agree requirements for new or changed services in Service Level Requirements, and manage and review them through the Service Lifecycle into SLAs for operational services
- Monitor and measure service performance achievements against targets within SLAs
- Collate, measure and improve customer satisfaction
- Produce service reports
- Conduct service reviews and instigate improvements within an overall SIP

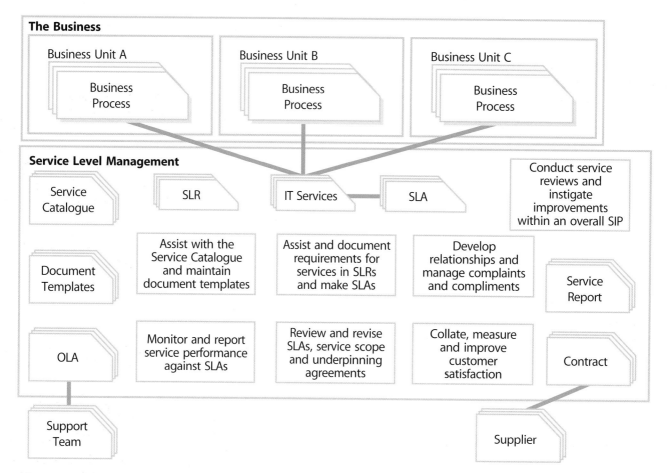

Figure 5.5 The Service Level Management process

- Review and revise SLAs, service scope, Operation Level Agreements, contracts and any other underpinning agreements
- Develop and document contacts and relationships with the business, customers and stakeholders and manage complaints and compliments
- Provide the appropriate management information to aid performance management and demonstrate service achievement.

5.5.2.4 Relationships

There are a number of sources of information that are relevant to the Service Level Management process. These include business information such as Business Impact Analysis and business requirements, the strategies, policies and constraints from Service Strategy, the Service Portfolio and Service Catalogue, change information from the Change Management process, information on the relationships between the business services, the supporting services and the technology from the Configuration Management System as well as other inputs, including advice, information and input from any of the other processes (e.g. Incident Management, Capacity Management and Availability Management).

5.5.3 Supplier Management

Brigitte steps out to the corridor from her room and bumps into the electrician Jacob who is preparing to install electronic card key locks on all the guest room doors. The hotel manager comes by to give some last instructions and when he makes a sign to leave again Brigitte asks him: 'Why don't you install the card system yourself?' The manager answers: 'This hotel is much too small to employ an electrician of its own. In this town there are only four independent electricians. Of these one has a very bad reputation; we have tried the other three. Of those we have had the best experiences with Jacob. Some of the things we like about Jacob are that he always keeps us informed about the progress of his work as well as any risks for delays. He takes responsibility for the job and strives to obtain the best result for the hotel.'

As a result of the evaluation of his work, the hotel has established a three-year contract with Jacob. The contract allows the hotel to call Jacob at all hours whenever a problem has to be resolved. On the other hand, Jacob knows that he is the hotel's first choice whenever an electrician is needed.

5.5.3.1 Goals and objectives

■ To manage suppliers and the services they supply, to provide seamless quality of IT service to the business, ensuring value for money is obtained

■ To ensure that Underpinning Contracts and agreements with suppliers are aligned to business needs and managed through their lifecycle
■ To manage relationships with suppliers
■ To maintain a supplier policy and a supporting Supplier and Contract Database.

5.5.3.2 Basic concepts

Supplier and Contract Database

In order to achieve consistency and effectiveness in the implementation of the policy, a Supplier and Contract Database (SCD) should be established, together with clearly defined roles and responsibilities.

> **Definition**
>
> A **Supplier and Contract Database** (SCD) is a database or structured document used to manage supplier contracts throughout their lifecycle. The SCD contains key attributes of all contracts with suppliers, and should be part of the Service Knowledge Management System (SMKS).

Ideally the SCD should form an integrated element of a comprehensive Configuration Management System (CMS) and SKMS, recording all supplier and contract details, together with details of the types of services or products provided by each supplier, and all other information and relationships.

The services provided by suppliers will also form a key part of the Service Portfolio and the Service Catalogue. The relationship between the supporting services and the IT and business services they support are key to providing quality IT services.

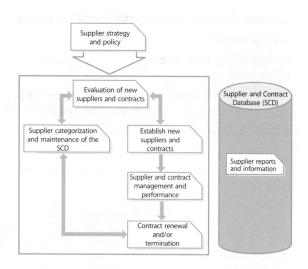

Figure 5.6 The Supplier Management process

The Supplier Management process

All Supplier Management process activity should be driven by a supplier strategy and policy from Service Strategy (Figure 5.6).

5.5.4 Capacity Management

Brigitte decides to take a walk and approaches the reception desk to leave her key. In front of her a man is asking for a room for one night without booking. Regrettably the receptionist can't offer any vacant rooms.

As Brigitte plans to come back to Switzerland next month she wants to ensure that she will be able to stay at the hotel. Consequently she asks the receptionist if there is cause for concern. The receptionist replies: 'If you make a reservation a few days ahead there's usually no problem. It is only a few weeks a year where we have to turn customers away from the hotel.'

'Why don't you expand the hotel then?'

'Because the occupancy until now hasn't been high enough to justify the investment. But based on the trend over the last five years and the town plans for expanding the nearby industrial area, the hotel has now planned for a new wing with rooms to be ready in two years from now. The construction will start in a few months' time.'

5.5.4.1 Goals and objectives

- To ensure that cost-justifiable capacity in all areas of IT always exists and is matched to the current and future agreed needs of the business, in a timely manner
- To produce and maintain an appropriate and up-to-date Capacity Plan, which reflects the current and future needs of the business
- To ensure that service performance achievements meet or exceed all of their agreed performance targets
- To assist with the diagnosis and resolution of capacity-related incidents and problems and assessment of the impact of all changes on capacity and resources.

5.5.4.2 Basic concepts

Keeping the balance

Capacity Management is essentially a balancing act:

- Balancing costs against resources needed
- Balancing supply against demand.

Capacity Plan

One of the key activities of Capacity Management is to produce a plan that documents the current levels of resource utilization and service performance and forecasts the future requirements for new resources to support the IT services that underpin the business activities. The plan should indicate clearly any assumptions made. It should also include any recommendations quantified in terms of resource required, cost, benefits, impact etc.

> **Definition**
>
> A **Capacity Plan** is used to manage the resources required to deliver services. The plan contains scenarios for different predictions of business demand, and costed options to deliver the agreed service level targets.

The production and maintenance of a Capacity Plan should occur at predefined intervals. It is, essentially, an investment plan and should therefore be published annually, in line with the business or budget lifecycle, and completed before the start of negotiations on future budgets.

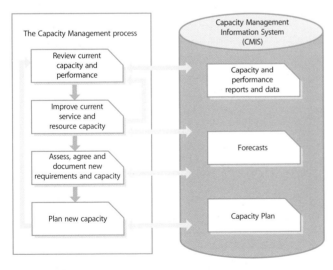

Figure 5.7 The Capacity Management process

Business, Service and Component Capacity Management

The overall Capacity Management process (Figure 5.7) is continually trying to match resources and capacity cost-effectively to the ever-changing needs and requirements of the business. This requires tuning and optimization of current resources and effective estimation and planning of future resources.

The Capacity Management process consists of three sub-processes:

- The Business Capacity Management sub-process translates business needs and plans into requirements for service and IT infrastructure
- The Service Capacity Management sub-process focuses on the management, control and prediction of the end-to-end performance and capacity of the operational IT services and their workloads
- The Component Capacity Management sub-process focuses on the management, control and prediction of the performance, utilization and capacity of individual components.

5.5.5 Availability Management

5.5.5.1 Goals and objectives

- To ensure that the level of service availability delivered in all services is matched to or exceeds the current and future agreed needs of the business, in a cost-effective manner
- To produce and maintain an up-to-date Availability Plan, which reflects the needs of the business
- To assist with the diagnosis and resolution of availability-related incidents and problems, and assessment of the impact of all changes on availability

■ To ensure that proactive improvements to service availability are implemented wherever possible.

5.5.5.2 Basic concepts

Availability

> **Definition**
>
> **Availability** is the ability of a service, component or CI to perform its agreed function when required.

Availability is usually calculated as a percentage. This calculation is often based on agreed service time and downtime. It is best practice to calculate availability using measurements of the business output of the IT service. It is often measured and reported as Mean Time Between Failures (MTBF).

Reliability

> **Definition**
>
> **Reliability** is a measure of how long a service, component or Configuration Item (CI) can perform its agreed function without interruption.

The reliability of the service can be improved by increasing the reliability of individual components or by increasing the resilience of the service to individual component failure (increasing the

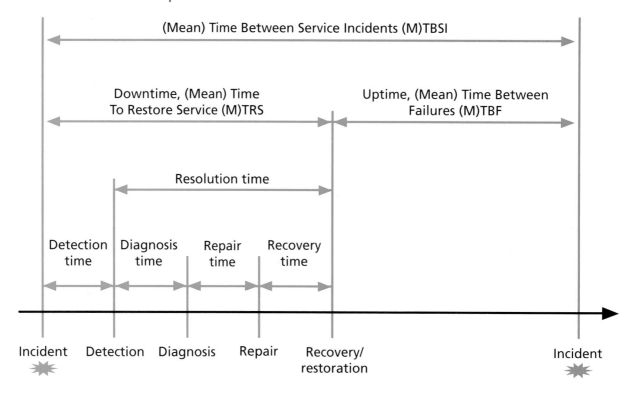

Figure 5.8 The expanded incident lifecycle

component redundancy, e.g. by using load-balancing techniques).

It is often measured and reported as Mean Time Between Service Incidents (MTBSI).

Maintainability

> **Definition**
>
> **Maintainability** is a measure of how quickly and effectively a service, component or Configuration Item (CI) can be restored to normal working after a failure.

Maintainability is measured and reported as Mean Time to Restore Service (MTRS).

Serviceability

> **Definition**
>
> **Serviceability** is the ability of a third-party supplier to meet the terms of their contract. Often this contract will include agreed levels of availability, reliability and/or maintainability for a supporting service or component.

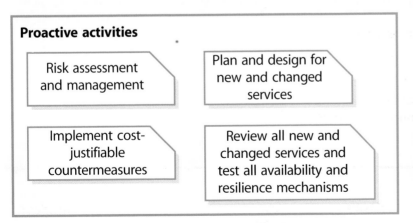

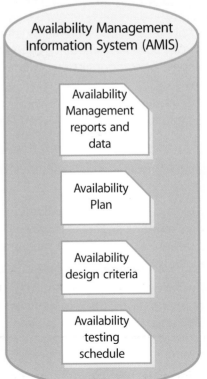

Figure 5.9 The Availability Management process

The expanded incident 'lifecycle'

A good technique to help with the technical analysis of incidents affecting the availability of IT services and components is to take an incident 'lifecycle' view.

Every incident passes through several major stages, which can be timed and measured. The time elapsed in these stages may vary considerably. Figure 5.8 illustrates the expanded incident lifecycle.

Service and Component Availability

Availability Management is completed at two interconnected levels:

- Service availability: involves all aspects of service availability and unavailability and the impact of component availability, or the potential impact of component unavailability, on service availability
- Component availability: involves all aspects of component availability and unavailability.

The Availability Management process

Availability Management should perform both reactive and proactive activities (Figure 5.9).

The reactive activities of Availability Management involve monitoring, measuring, analysis, reporting and reviewing all aspects of service and component availability.

The proactive activities consist of producing recommendations, plans and documents on design guidelines and criteria for new and changed services, and the continual improvement of service and reduction of risk in existing services wherever it can be cost-justified. These are key aspects to be considered within Service Design activities.

5.5.6 Service Continuity Management

Brigitte notices that the receptionist seems sad and asks him if he is all right. He hesitates before he answers. But then he tells her that one of his good friends, a waiter at another hotel, has just lost his job. The hotel was struck by a disaster – an avalanche destroyed most of the hotel. The disaster was managed very badly and no one seemed to be prepared for a situation like this. For example, there hadn't been any plan for re-housing the guests. As a result the customers had lost confidence in the hotel and after a short while the hotel went bankrupt, even though the insurance had covered the reconstruction of the hotel.

5.5.6.1 Goals and objectives

- To support the overall Business Continuity Management process by ensuring that the required service facilities can be resumed within required, and agreed, business timescales
- To maintain a set of IT service continuity plans and IT recovery plans that support the overall Business Continuity Plans of an organization
- To ensure that all continuity plans are maintained in line with changing business impacts, requirements and risks through regular Business Impact Analysis (BIA) exercises and risk assessments
- To ensure that appropriate continuity and recovery mechanisms are put in place to meet agreed business continuity targets.

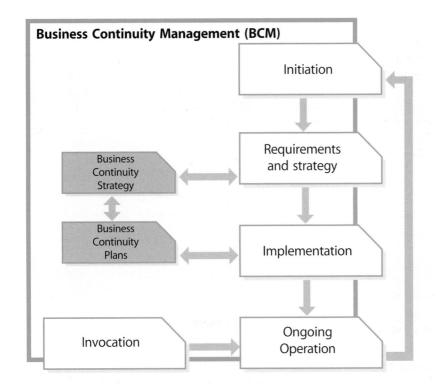

Figure 5.10 The Service Continuity Management process

5.5.6.2 Basic concepts

Business Continuity Management and Business Continuity Plans

Business Continuity Management is the business process responsible for managing risks that could seriously impact the business. Business Continuity Management safeguards the interests of key stakeholders, reputation, brand and value-creating activities. The Business Continuity Management process involves reducing risks to an acceptable level and planning for the recovery of business processes should a disruption to the business occur. Business Continuity Management sets the objectives, scope and requirements for IT Service Continuity Management.

Figure 5.10 shows the role played within the Service Continuity Management process of Business Continuity Management.

Service Continuity Management is a cyclical process throughout the lifecycle to ensure that once service continuity and recovery plans have been developed, they are kept aligned with Business Continuity Plans and business priorities.

A **Business Continuity Plan** is a plan defining the steps required to restore business processes following a disruption. The plan will also identify the triggers for invocation, people to be involved, communications etc. IT Service Continuity Plans form a significant part of Business Continuity Plans.

Business Impact Analysis

The purpose of a Business Impact Analysis (BIA) is to quantify the impact to the business that loss of service would have. This impact could be a 'hard' impact that can be precisely identified – such as financial loss – or a 'soft' impact – such as public relations, morale, health and safety or loss of competitive advantage. The BIA will identify the most important services to the organization and will therefore be a key input to the strategy.

Business Impact Analysis (BIA) is the activity in Business Continuity Management that identifies vital business functions and their dependencies. These dependencies may include suppliers, people, other business processes, IT services etc.

BIA defines the recovery requirements for IT services. These requirements include recovery time objectives, recovery point objectives and minimum service level targets for each IT service.

Risk analysis

The second driver in determining IT Service Continuity Management requirements is the likelihood that a disaster or other serious service disruption will actually occur. This is an assessment of the level of threat and the extent to which an organization is vulnerable to that threat. Risk analysis can also be used in assessing and reducing the chance of normal operational incidents and is a technique used by Availability Management to ensure the required availability and reliability levels can be maintained.

Risk analysis is the assessment of the risks that may give rise to service disruption or security violation.

Risk management is concerned with identifying appropriate risk responses or cost-justifiable countermeasures to combat those risks. A standard methodology, such as the Management of Risk (M_o_R), should be used to assess and manage risks within an organization.

5.5.7 Information Security Management

Brigitte meets the hotel manager in the lobby and they continue their little chat on the installation of the electronic card key system. She wonders why a peaceful little hotel in the Alps is mounting a card key system.

He takes a deep breath before he answers, but as she promises not to tell anyone he continues: 'There have been a number of thefts from the hotel, mainly cigarettes from the restaurant but also other objects. As a result the management evaluated the overall hotel security and made a plan for improvements. Based on the plan a security policy was developed and the management team have committed to ensure that it is implemented within a reasonable timeframe. A part of the implementation is to restrict the physical access to the hotel.'

The manager expresses his hope that the increased physical security together with some of the other measures in the security policy will eliminate the thefts. He therefore looks forward to evaluating the results of the initiatives in six months.

5.5.7.1 Goals and objectives

- To align information security with business security and ensure that information security is effectively managed in all Service Management activities
- To ensure that the information security risks are appropriately managed and enterprise information resources are used responsibly
- To protect the interests of those relying on information, and the systems and communications that deliver the information, from harm resulting from failures of availability, confidentiality and integrity.

5.5.7.2 Basic concepts

Security Framework

The Information Security Management process and framework will generally consist of:

- An Information Security Policy and specific security policies that address each aspect of strategy, controls and regulation; the policies should be widely available to all customers and users
- An Information Security Management System (ISMS), containing the standards, management procedures and guidelines supporting the Information Security Policies
- A comprehensive Security Strategy closely linked to the business objectives, strategies and plans
- An effective security organization
- A set of security controls to support the Information Security Policy
- The management of security risks

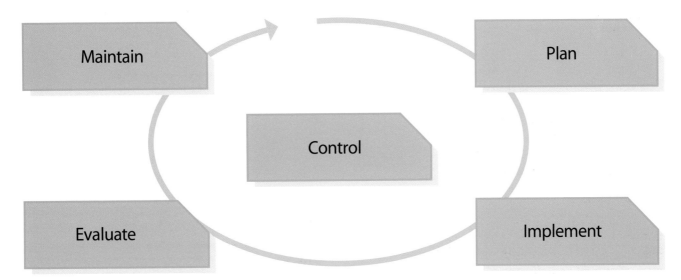

Figure 5.11 Framework for managing information security

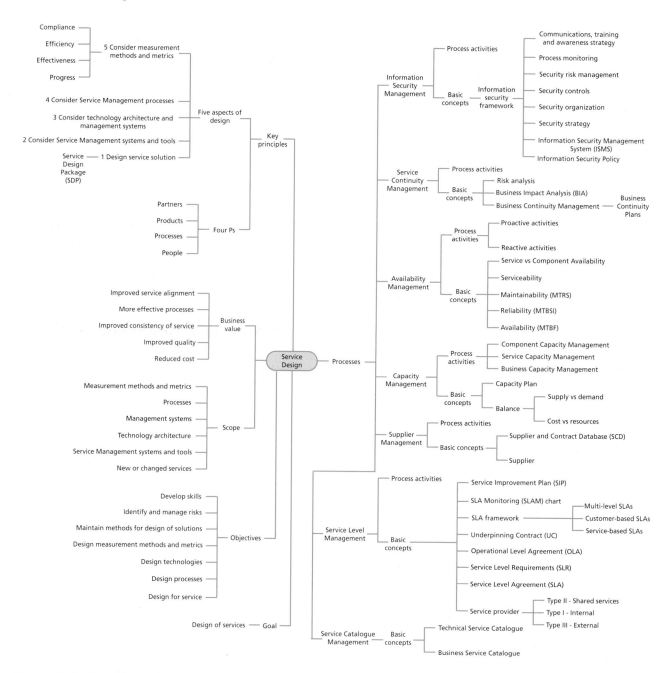

Figure 5.12 Overview of Chapter 5 (Service Design)

- Monitoring of processes to ensure compliance and effectiveness
- A communications, training and awareness strategy and a plan for security.

Information Security Management System

The framework of the Information Security Management System (ISMS) in turn provides a basis for the development of a cost-effective information security programme that supports the business objectives.

> **Definition**
>
> The **Information Security Management System** (ISMS) is a framework to design, implement, manage, maintain and enforce information security processes and controls systematically and consistently throughout an organization.

The ISMS framework in Figure 5.11 shows an approach that is widely used and is based on the advice and guidance described in ISO/IEC 27001.

Information Security Policy

Information Security Management activities should be focused on and driven by an overall Information Security Policy and a set of underpinning specific security policies. The policy should cover all areas of security, be appropriate and meet the needs of the business.

The security policies should be widely available to all customers and users, and their compliance should be referred to in all Service Level Requirements, SLAs, contracts and agreements. The policies should be authorized by top executive management within the business and IT, and compliance to them should be endorsed regularly. All security policies should be reviewed – and, where necessary, revised – at least annually.

5.6 SAMPLE QUESTIONS

1 Which of the following describes the four Ps of Service Design?

   a A process for the design of effective services

   b The planning, perspective, position and people aspects of Service Design

   c Questions that should be asked when reviewing design specifications

   d The people, partner, product and process elements to be considered in the design of services.

2 Which of the following statements about Supplier Management is INCORRECT?

   a Supplier Management negotiates Operational Level Agreements (OLAs) with internal groups to support the delivery of services.

   b Supplier Management ensures that suppliers meet business expectations.

   c Supplier Management maintains information in a Supplier and Contract Database.

   d Supplier Management negotiates external agreements to support the delivery of services.

3 The three sub-processes of Capacity Management are:

   a Business Capacity Management, Service Capacity Management and Component Capacity Management

   b Supplier Capacity Management, Service Capacity Management and Component Capacity Management c Supplier Capacity Management, Service Capacity Management and Technology Capacity Management

   d Business Capacity Management, Technology Capacity Management and Component Capacity Management.

4   Which of the following statements is NOT an objective of Service Design?

   a To design services to satisfy business objectives

   b To design the organizational structure for the operation of a high-quality service

   c To design the measurement methods and metrics in order to assess the effectiveness of Service Design

   d To design efficient and effective processes for the design, transition, operation and improvement of high-quality IT services.

5   A Service Level Agreement is BEST described as:

   a The organization supplying services to one or more internal customers or external customers

   b An agreement between a service provider and the customers of the service that details the services, their targets and the responsibilities of both parties

   c An underpinning agreement between an IT service provider and another part of the same organization that assists with the provision of services

   d An agreement between a service provider and the customers of the service that details the services, their targets and the responsibilities of the service provider.

Service Transition

6

6 Service Transition

Service Transition moves services and service changes into operational use. Service Transition achieves this by receiving a new or changed Service Design Package from the Service Design stage, testing it to ensure it meets the needs of the business, and deploying it within the production environment.

As the planning and design of the new conference services progresses, the project manager has started thinking about the implementation phase. He has already drafted some activities that he expects to include in the transition phase:

- Plan the implementation in detail
- Assemble and build the designed facilities
- Train the staff in the facilities and processes
- Test that the conference facilities function as they are intended to
- Inspect that the facilities conform to the requirements from the local businesses as well as regulations put forward by the local authorities.

6.1 GOALS AND OBJECTIVES

The main goals of Service Transition are to:

- Transition services to and from the live environment, managing required resources and risks and ensuring that agreed warranty and utility are delivered
- Set customer expectations of how the performance and use of a new or changed service can be used to enable business change

- Enable the business change project or customer to integrate a release into their business processes and services
- Ensure that the service can be used in accordance with the requirements and constraints specified within the service requirements.

The main objectives of Service Transition are to:

- Plan and manage the resources to establish successfully a new or changed service into production within the predicted cost, quality and time estimates
- Ensure there is minimal unpredicted impact on the production services, operations and support organization
- Increase the customer, user and Service Management staff satisfaction with the Service Transition practices
- Increase proper use of the services and underlying applications and technology solutions
- Provide clear and comprehensive plans that enable the customer and business change projects to align their activities with the Service Transition plans.

6.2 SCOPE

The scope of Service Transition (Figure 6.1) includes the management and coordination of the resources to package, build, test and deploy a release into production and to establish the new or changed service as specified in the customer and stakeholder requirements.

The following activities are excluded from the scope of Service Transition best practices:

■ Minor modifications to the production services and environment, e.g. replacement of a failed PC or registration of a new user

■ Ongoing Continual Service Improvements that do not significantly impact on the services or service provider's capability to deliver the services.

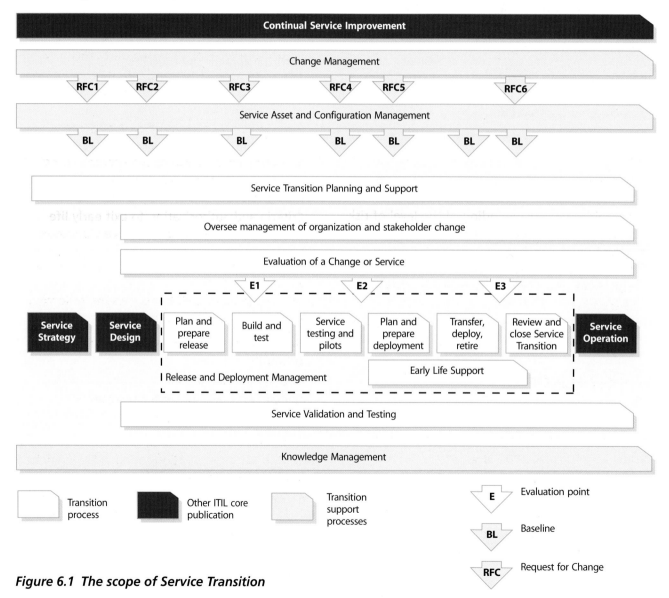

Figure 6.1 The scope of Service Transition

Service Transition activities are shown in the white boxes in Figure 6.1. The dark boxes represent activities in the other stages of the Service Lifecycle.

The following lifecycle processes in the Service Transition stage support all lifecycle stages:

- Change Management
- Service Asset and Configuration Management
- Knowledge Management.

6.3 BUSINESS VALUE

Effective Service Transition provides the following benefits:

- It enables high volumes of change and releases for the business
- It provides an understanding of the level of risk during and after change, e.g. service outage, disruption, re-work
- It aligns the new or changed service with the customer's business requirements and business operations
- It ensures that customers and users can use the new or changed service effectively.

6.4 KEY PRINCIPLES

6.4.1 Service Transition policies

Formal policies for Service Transition should be defined, documented and approved. Among these a release policy should be defined for one or more services and among other things include:

- The unique identification, numbering and naming conventions for different types of release, together with a description

- The roles and responsibilities at each stage in the release and deployment process
- The expected frequency for each type of release
- The approach for accepting and grouping changes into a release, e.g. how enhancements are prioritized for inclusion
- The mechanism to automate the build, installation and release distribution processes to improve re-use, repeatability and efficiency
- Details of how the configuration baseline for the release is captured and verified against the actual release contents
- Exit and entry criteria and authority for acceptance of the release into each Service Transition stage and into the controlled test, training, disaster recovery and production environments
- Criteria and authorization to exit early life support and hand over to Service Operation.

6.5 PROCESSES

The ITIL Foundation syllabus covers the following Service Transition processes:

- Service Asset and Configuration Management (SACM)
- Change Management
- Release and Deployment Management
- Knowledge Management.

In addition the Service Transition book includes the Transition Planning and Support, Service Validation and Testing Management and Evaluation Management processes, but as these are not part of the ITIL Foundation syllabus they will not be further discussed.

6.5.1 Service Asset and Configuration Management

6.5.1.1 Goals and objectives

- To support efficient and effective business and Service Management processes by providing accurate configuration information to enable people to make decisions at the right time, e.g. to authorize changes and releases, or to resolve incidents and problems faster
- To provide a logical model of the services, assets and different components (physical, logical etc.) and their relationships needed to deliver these services
- To define and control the components of services and infrastructure and maintain accurate configuration records
- To enable an organization to comply with corporate governance requirements, control its asset base, optimize its costs, manage change and releases effectively, and resolve incidents and problems faster.

6.5.1.2 Basic concepts

Configuration Item

> **Definition**
>
> A **Configuration Item** (CI) is any component that needs to be managed in order to deliver an IT service.

Information about each CI is recorded in a configuration record within the Configuration Management System (CMS) and is maintained throughout its lifecycle by Configuration Management. CIs are under the control of Change Management.

CIs may vary widely in complexity, size and type, ranging from an entire service or system, including all hardware, software, documentation and support staff, to a single software module or a minor hardware component.

There will be a variety of CIs. The following categories may help to identify them:

- **Service Lifecycle CIs**   Such as the business case, Service Management plans, Service Lifecycle plans, Service Design Package, release and change plans, test plans
- **Service CIs**   Such as Service Capability assets (management, organization, processes, knowledge, people), service resource assets (financial capital, systems, applications, information, data, infrastructure and facilities, financial capital, people), service model, service package, release package, service acceptance criteria
- **Organization CIs**   Such as an organization's business strategy or other policies
- **Internal CIs**   Comprising those delivered by individual projects, including assets such as hardware and software that are required to deliver and maintain the service and infrastructure
- **External CIs**   Such as external customer requirements and agreements, releases from suppliers or sub-contractors, and external services.

Configuration baseline

A configuration baseline is the configuration of a service, product or infrastructure that serves as the basis for further activities and that can be changed only through formal change procedures. It captures the structure, contents and details of a configuration and represents a set of Configuration Items that are related to each other.

Establishing a baseline provides the ability to:

■ Mark a milestone in the development of a service, e.g. Service Design baseline
■ Build a service component from a defined set of inputs
■ Change or rebuild a specific version at a later date

■ Assemble all relevant components in readiness for a change or release
■ Provide the basis for a configuration audit and backout, e.g. after a change.

Configuration model

Configuration Management delivers a logical model of the services, assets and infrastructure by recording the relationships between CIs, as shown in Figure 6.2. This enables other processes to access valuable information such as to:

■ Assess the impact and cause of incidents and problems
■ Assess the impact of proposed changes
■ Plan and design new or changed services
■ Plan technology refresh and software upgrades

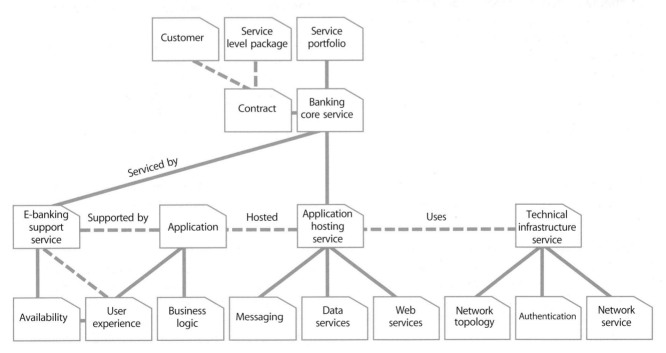

Figure 6.2 Example of a logical configuration model

■ Plan release and deployment packages and migrate service assets to different locations and service centres

■ Optimize asset utilization and costs, e.g. consolidate data centres, reduce variations.

Configuration Management System

> **Definition**
>
> A **Configuration Management System** (CMS) is a set of tools and databases that are used to manage a service provider's configuration data.

The CMS will hold details of all of the components of the IT infrastructure as well as the relationships between these components.

The CMS maintains the relationships between all service components and any related incidents and problems, known errors, and change and release documentation, and it may also contain corporate data about employees, suppliers, locations and business units, customers and users.

At the data level, the CMS may take data from several physical Configuration Management Databases (CMDBs), which together constitute a federated CMDB. Other data sources will also

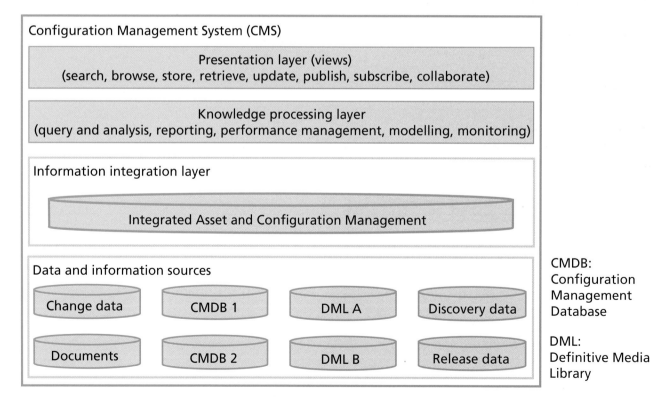

CMDB: Configuration Management Database

DML: Definitive Media Library

Figure 6.3 Example of a Configuration Management System

plug into the CMS, such as the Definitive Media Libraries. The CMS will provide access to data in asset inventories wherever possible rather than duplicating data (Figure 6.3).

Definition

A **Configuration Management Database** (CMDB) is a database used to store configuration records throughout their lifecycle. The Configuration Management System maintains one or more CMDBs, and each CMDB stores attributes of CIs, and relationships with other CIs.

The CMS typically contains configuration data and information that is combined into an integrated set of views for different stakeholders through the Service Lifecycle. It therefore needs to be based on appropriate web, reporting and database technologies that provide flexible and powerful visualization and mapping tools, interrogation and reporting facilities.

The CMS is maintained by Configuration Management and is used by all Service Management processes.

Later that evening in the restaurant, Brigitte overhears a conversation between the hotel manager and the chef. The manager is dissatisfied with the fact that the chef doesn't take his administrative duties seriously enough. It turns out that the hotel maintains a database of all relevant equipment, people, suppliers and processes that are used to provide the services. The staff are supposed to register selected assets such as rooms, beds and restaurant tables and the impact of these items on the services and the guests in the database every time they make a change to an item.

Over the years, the hotel has gained much experience in which data (such as equipment, people, suppliers and processes) it is important to register and maintain. Currently the configuration database includes information about:

■ Guests
■ Staff members
■ Guest rooms
■ Beds
■ Meeting rooms
■ Conference equipment
■ Restaurant tables
■ Suppliers
■ IT applications
■ Processes
■ Functions (reception, kitchen etc.)
■ Reservations of rooms (relations between rooms and guests) – it is possible to identify the vacant and reserved rooms and to see which rooms a guest stayed in during previous visits
■ Reservation of tables (relations between tables and guests)
■ Ownership and responsibility (relations between staff members and other items)
■ Allocation of staff (relations between staff members and functions or roles).

This information makes it possible to manage the provided services and analyse the impact of faults or changes to underpinning items.

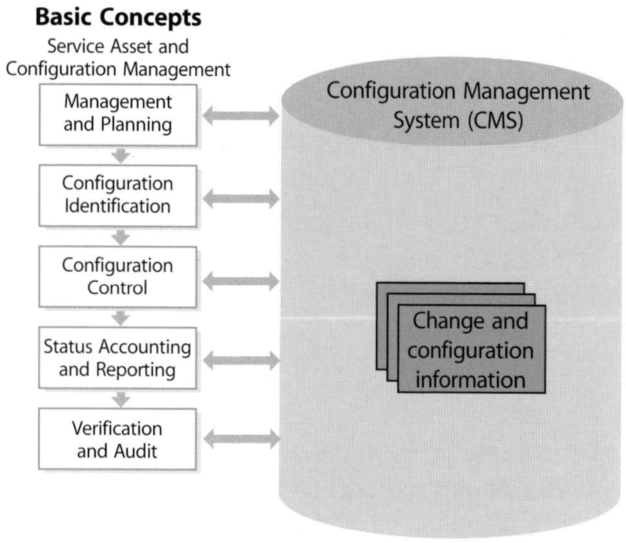

Basic Concepts
Service Asset and
Configuration Management

Figure 6.4 The Service Asset and Configuration Management process

- The roles and responsibilities of the owner or custodian for CI type at each stage of its lifecycle
- **Configuration control** Ensuring that there are adequate control mechanisms over CIs while maintaining a record of changes to status, approvals, location and ownership
- **Status accounting and reporting** Each CI will have one or more discrete states through which it can progress. The significance of each state should be defined in terms of what use can be made of the CI
- **Verification and audit** Checking that the physical CIs exist and that documentation is accurate
- **Information management** Backup copies of the Configuration Management System (CMS) should be taken regularly and securely stored.

6.5.1.3 Process activities

High-level activities for Service Asset and Configuration Management are shown in Figure 6.4.

- **Management and planning** Deciding what level of Configuration Management is required for a service or a change project. This is documented in a Configuration Management plan
- **Configuration identification** When planning configuration identification, it is important to define:
  - How the classes and types of assets and Configuration Items are to be selected, grouped, classified and defined by appropriate characteristics
  - The approach to identification, uniquely naming and labelling all the components of interest and the relationships between them

6.5.1.4 Relationships

By its very nature – as the single virtual repository of configuration data and information for IT Service Management – Service Asset and Configuration Management supports and interfaces with every other process and activity to some degree. Some of the more noteworthy interfaces are:

- **Change Management** Identifying the impact of proposed changes
- **Financial management** Capturing key financial information such as cost, depreciation methods, owner and user (for budgeting and cost allocation), maintenance and repair costs
- **IT Service Continuity Management** Awareness of assets the business services depend on; control of key spares and software
- **Incident and Problem Management** Providing and maintaining key diagnostic information;

maintenance and provision of data to the Service Desk

- **Availability Management** Detecting points of failure.

The relationship with change and release and deployment is synergistic, with these processes benefiting greatly from a single coordinated planning approach. Configuration control is synonymous with change control – understanding and capturing updates to the infrastructure and services.

6.5.2 Change Management

The very first time Brigitte stayed at the hotel no internet connection was available for the guests. Brigitte had been quite surprised as the majority of the hotel guests were business people like herself. Upon her departure she had told the receptionist that she had missed that service and the receptionist had made a note of her request and told her that she had just received the same request from one of their travel agency customers.

To Brigitte's surprise she got a call from the hotel when she came home; the man who called told her that he was assessing and evaluating her suggestion for an internet connection. He had been talking to a number of people, including technicians to assess the possible technical solutions and the Financial Manager to raise funding. Now he wanted to listen to a potential customer's viewpoint. He asked her some questions on the reason for her request and whether she as a guest would be willing to pay for the service.

When she came back to the hotel a year later there was a wireless internet connection in her room. She only had to buy an access code at the reception.

And once more she received – again to her surprise – a call from the hotel when she came home; this time they wanted to know whether the internet connection met her expectations or whether anything needed to be changed from Brigitte's perspective.

6.5.2.1 Goals and objectives

- To respond to the customer's changing business requirements while maximizing value and reducing incidents, disruption and re-work
- To respond to the business and IT requests for change that will integrate the services with the business needs
- To ensure that changes are recorded, evaluated, authorized, prioritized, planned, tested, implemented, documented and reviewed in a controlled manner.

6.5.2.2 Basic concepts

Change

Definition

A **change** is the addition, modification or removal of anything that could have an effect on services. The scope should include services, Configuration Items (CIs), processes, documentation etc.

Change types

Changes can be divided into three types:

1 Normal change

Normal changes go through the full assessment, authorization and implementation stages and typically includes change requests such as:

- RFC to the Service Portfolio
- RFC to a service
- Project change proposal
- User access request
- Operational activity.

For different change types there are often specific procedures, e.g. for impact assessment and change authorization.

2 Standard change

A standard change is a pre-approved change that is low risk, relatively common and follows a procedure or work instruction, e.g. a password reset or provision of standard equipment to a new employee. RFCs are not always required to implement a standard change, and they may be logged and tracked using a different mechanism, e.g. a Service Request. Often, service operational maintenance changes are standard changes.

The crucial elements of a standard change are that:

- There is a defined trigger to initiate the RFC
- The tasks are well known, documented and proven
- Authority is effectively given in advance
- Budgetary approval will typically be preordained or within the control of the standard change requester
- They are usually low risk, and always contain well-understood risk.

3 Emergency change

Emergency change is reserved only for highly critical changes that must be introduced as soon as possible, e.g. changes needed to restore failed high availability or widespread service failure, or changes that will prevent such a failure from imminently occurring.

In an emergency situation it may not be possible to convene a full CAB meeting. Where CAB approval is required, this will be provided by the Emergency CAB (ECAB).

Change process models and workflows

Organizations will find it helpful to predefine change process models – and apply them to appropriate changes when they occur. A process model is a way of predefining the steps that should be taken to handle a particular type of change in an agreed way.

The change process model includes:

- The steps that should be taken to handle the change, including handling issues and unexpected events
- The chronological order these steps should be taken in, with any dependences or co-processing defined
- Responsibilities: who should do what
- Timescales and thresholds for completion of the actions
- Escalation procedures: who should be contacted and when.

The seven Rs of Change Management

The following questions must be answered for all changes. Without this information, the impact assessment cannot be completed, and the balance of risk and benefit to the live service will not be understood:

1 Who **raised** the change?

2 What is the **reason** for the change?

3 What is the **return** required from the change?

4 What are the **risks** involved in the change?

5 What **resources** are required to deliver the change?

6 Who is **responsible** for the build, test and implementation of the change?

7 What is the **relationship** between this change and other changes?

Remediation planning

No change should be approved without having explicitly addressed the question of what to do if it is not successful. Ideally, there will be a back-out plan, which will restore the organization to its initial situation, often through the reloading of a baselined set of Configuration Items, especially software and data. However, not all changes are reversible, in which case an alternative approach to remediation is required.

Change Advisory Board

The Change Advisory Board (CAB) is a group of people who advise the Change Manager in the assessment, prioritization and scheduling of changes.

As and when a CAB is convened, members should be chosen who are capable of ensuring that all changes within the scope of the CAB are adequately assessed from both a business and a technical viewpoint.

To achieve this, the CAB needs to include people with a clear understanding across the whole range of stakeholder needs. The Change Manager will normally chair the CAB, and potential members include:

- Customer(s)
- User manager(s)
- User group representative(s)
- Applications developers/maintainers
- Specialists/technical consultants
- Services and operations staff, e.g. Service Desk, test management, IT Service Continuity Management, security, capacity
- Facilities/office services staff (where changes may affect moves/accommodation and vice versa)
- Contractor's or third parties' representatives, e.g. in outsourcing situations
- Other parties as applicable to specific circumstances (e.g. police if traffic disruptions are likely, marketing if public products are affected).

When the need for emergency change arises, i.e. where there may not be time to convene the full CAB, it is necessary to identify a smaller organization with authority to make emergency decisions. This body is the Emergency Change Advisory Board (ECAB). Change procedures should specify how the composition of the CAB and ECAB will be determined in each instance.

6.5.2.3 Process activities

Overall Change Management activities include:

- Planning and controlling changes
- Change and release scheduling
- Communications

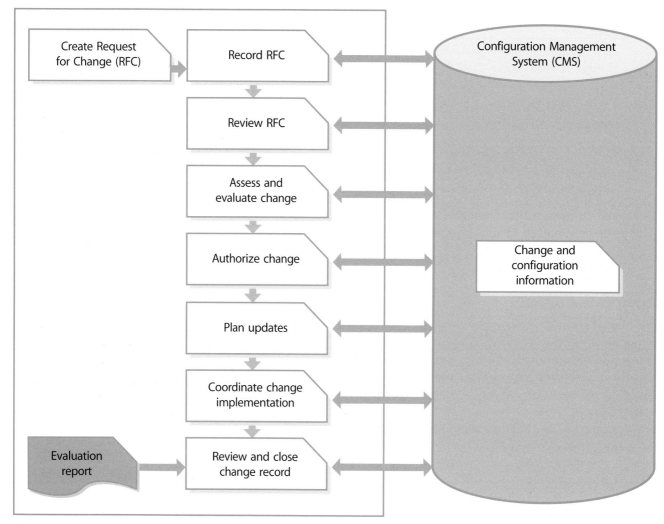

Figure 6.5 Example process flow for a normal change

- Change decision making and change authorization
- Ensuring there are remediation plans
- Measurement and control
- Management reporting
- Understanding the impact of change
- Continual improvement.

Typical activities in managing individual changes are to:

- Create and record changes
- Review and filter RFCs and the change proposal
- Assess and evaluate the change:

- Establish the appropriate level of change authority
- Establish relevant areas of interest (who should be involved in the CAB)
- Assess and evaluate the business justification, impact, cost, benefits and risk of changes
- Request independent evaluation of a change

■ Authorize the change:
  - Obtain authorization/rejection
  - Communicate the decision to all stakeholders, in particular the initiator of the RFC

■ Plan updates
■ Coordinate change implementation
■ Review and close each change.

See Figure 6.5.

6.5.2.4 Relationships

In order to be able to define clear boundaries, dependencies and rules, Change and Release Management should be integrated with processes used for organizational programmes or projects, Supplier Management and also suppliers' processes and procedures. There will be occasions when a proposed change will potentially have a wider impact on other parts of the organization (e.g. facilities or business operations), or vice versa, and the service change process must interface appropriately with other processes involved:

■ Programme and project management
■ Sourcing and partnering
■ Asset and Configuration Management
■ Problem Management
■ IT Service Continuity Management
■ Security Management
■ Capacity and Demand Management.

6.5.3 Release and Deployment Management

Brigitte was glad to find the new wireless internet connection service available the second time she visited the hotel. But she also wondered why she had to order a room with internet in advance and why the hotel hadn't just implemented the service in all rooms.

Jacob, who was assigned to implement the internet services, explained that the hotel had wanted to keep control of the deployment so they had chosen a phased approach, to ensure that one phase was a success before moving on to the next.

Actually the hotel started with a very small installation and had asked a few loyal customers to be test pilots. In the second phase the service had been available to guests who specifically asked for it. Now in the third phase they advertised the service and they were planning to roll out the service to all the remaining rooms – and to the reception area in a fourth phase if this phase went well.

6.5.3.1 Goals and objectives

■ To deploy releases into production and enable effective use of the service in order to deliver value to the customer
■ To ensure that there are clear and comprehensive release and deployment plans that enable the customer and business change projects to align their activities with these plans
■ To ensure that a release package can be built, installed, tested and deployed efficiently, successfully and on schedule

- To ensure that a new or changed service and its enabling systems, technology and organization are capable of delivering the agreed service requirements, i.e. utilities, warranties and service levels
- To transfer knowledge to customers and users to optimize their use of the service
- To transfer skills and knowledge to operations and support staff to enable them to deliver, support and maintain the service effectively and efficiently.

6.5.3.2 Basic concepts

Release and release unit

Definition

A **release** is a collection of hardware, software, documentation, processes or other components required to implement one or more approved changes to IT Services. The contents of each release are managed, tested and deployed as a single entity.

Definition

A **release unit** is a collection of components of an IT service that are normally released together according to an organization's release policy.

A release unit typically includes sufficient components to perform a useful function. For example, one release unit could be a desktop PC, including hardware, software, licences, documentation etc. Another release unit may be the complete payroll application, including IT Operations procedures and user training.

The unit may vary, depending on the types or items of service asset or service component, such as software and hardware. Figure 6.6 is a simplified example showing an IT service made up of systems and service assets, which are in turn made up of service components.

The general aim is to decide the most appropriate release unit level for each service asset or component. An organization may, for example, decide that the release unit for business-critical

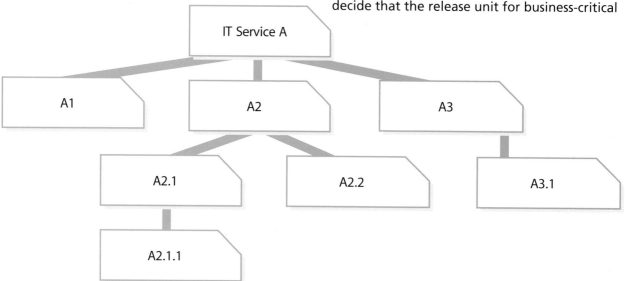

Figure 6.6 Simplified example of release units for an IT service

applications is the complete application in order to ensure that testing is comprehensive. The same organization may decide that a more appropriate release unit for a website is at the page level.

A release package may be a single release unit or a structured set of release units.

Definitive Media Library

> **Definition**
>
> A **Definitive Media Library** (DML) is one or more locations in which the definitive and approved versions of all software CIs are securely stored. The DML may also contain associated CIs such as licences and documentation.

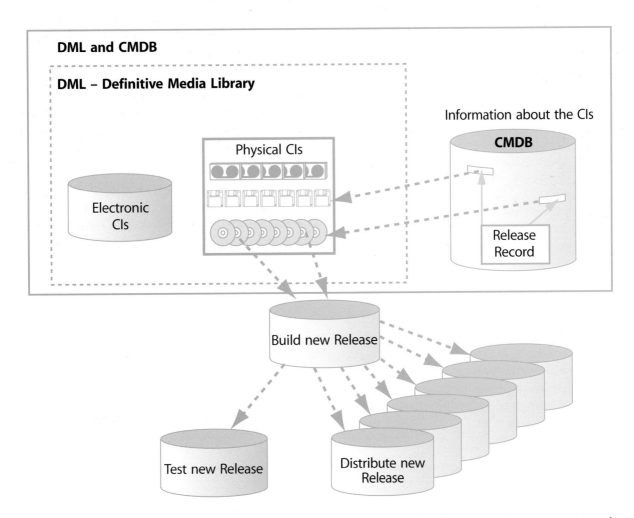

Figure 6.7 Relationship between the Definitive Media Library and the Configuration Management Database

The DML should include definitive copies of purchased software (along with licence documents or information) and software developed on site. Master copies of controlled documentation for a system are also stored in the DML in electronic form.

The DML will also include a physical store to hold master copies, e.g. a fireproof safe.

All software in the DML is under the control of Change and Release Management and is recorded in the Configuration Management System (Figure 6.7) strictly controlled by Service Asset and Configuration Management.

Release deployment options

Several options and combinations exist for deploying new releases to multiple locations:

- **Big bang**   The new or changed service is deployed to all user areas in one operation
- **Phased approach**   The service is deployed to a part of the user base initially, and then this operation is repeated for subsequent parts of the user base via a scheduled roll-out plan
- **A push approach**   The service component is deployed from the centre and pushed out to the target locations. The new or changed service is delivered into the user's environment at a time not of their choosing
- **A pull approach**   The software is made available in a central location but users are free to pull the software down to their own location at a time of their choosing or when a user workstation restarts
- **Automation**   This will help to ensure repeatability and consistency
- **Manual mechanism**   If used, it is important to monitor and measure the impact of many repeated manual activities as they are likely to be inefficient and error-prone. Too many manual activities will slow down the release team and create resource/capacity issues that affect the service levels.

The release and deployment process

Any significant new or changed service or service offering will require the deployment stage to consider the full range of elements comprising that service – infrastructure, hardware, software, applications, documentation, knowledge etc. Effectively this means the deployment will contain sub-deployments for elements comprising the service, as illustrated in Figure 6.8. The combination, relationship and interdependencies of these components will require careful and considered planning. Significant deployments will be complex projects in their own right.

6.5.4 Knowledge Management

Brigitte sits at her balcony enjoying the beautiful sunset over the mountains and it reminds her of the first time she stayed in this suite. She was asked to visit the factory at short notice, but she hoped that the hotel still had rooms available when she called the hotel. The receptionist could see from the registry that Brigitte often stayed at the hotel and that all the rooms of her choice were booked, so he offered her a discount. At the same time he made a reservation in the restaurant for her on the first night. She ended up with the suite, and since then she has always ordered it if available.

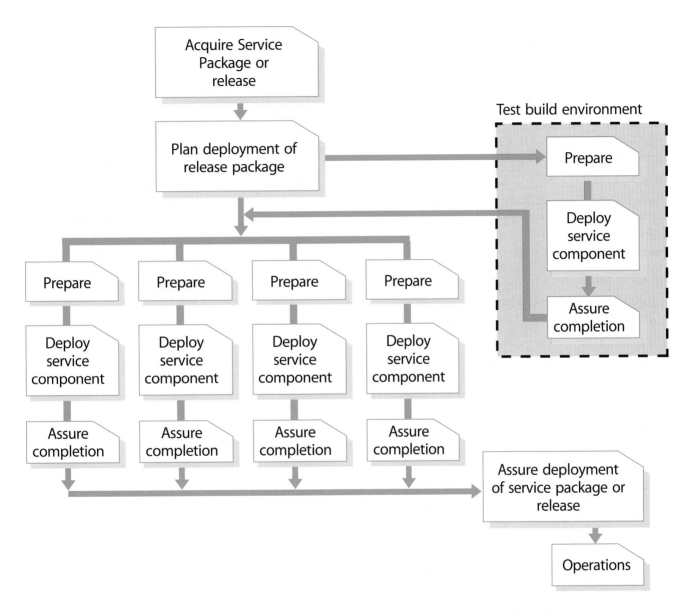

Figure 6.8 The release and deployment process: coordinating the deployment of service components

6.5.4.1 Goals and objectives

- To ensure that the right information is delivered to the appropriate place or competent person at the right time to enable informed decision making
- To enable organizations to improve the quality of management decision making by ensuring that reliable and secure information and data are available throughout the Service Lifecycle
- To enable the service provider to be more efficient and improve quality of service, increase satisfaction and reduce the cost of service
- To ensure that staff have a clear and common understanding of the value that their services provide to customers and the ways in which benefits are realized from the use of those services.

6.5.4.2 Basic concepts

Data to wisdom

Knowledge Management is typically displayed within the DIKW (data, information, knowledge and wisdom) structure (Figure 6.9). The use of these terms is set out below:

- **Data** is a set of discrete facts about events. Most organizations capture significant amounts of data in highly structured databases such as Service Management and Configuration Management tools/systems and databases
- **Information** comes from providing context to data. Information is typically stored in semi-structured content such as documents, e-mail and multimedia

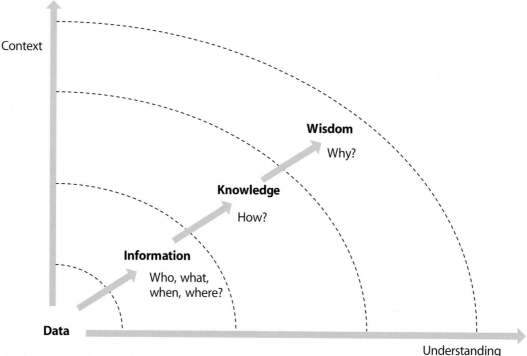

Figure 6.9 The DIKW (data, information, knowledge and wisdom) model

- **Knowledge** is composed of the tacit experiences, ideas, insights, values and judgements of individuals. People gain knowledge from both their own and their peers' expertise, as well as from the analysis of information (and data). Through the synthesis of these elements, new knowledge is created
- **Wisdom** gives the ultimate discernment of the material and means having the application and contextual awareness to provide a strong common sense judgement.

Service Knowledge Management System

> **Definition**
>
> A **Service Knowledge Management System** (SKMS) is a set of tools and databases that are used to manage knowledge and information. The SKMS stores, manages, updates and presents all information that a service provider needs to manage the full lifecycle of services.

The SKMS includes the Configuration Management System (CMS) and Configuration Management Databases, as well as other tools and databases.

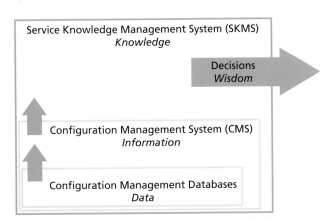

Figure 6.10 Example of a Service Knowledge Management System

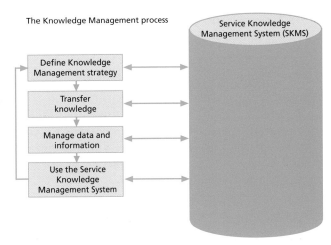

Figure 6.11 The Knowledge Management process

However, clearly the Service Knowledge Management System is a broader concept that covers a much wider base of knowledge, for example:

- The experience of staff
- Records of peripheral matters, e.g. user numbers and an organization's performance figures
- Supplier and partners' requirements, abilities and expectations
- Typical and anticipated user skill levels.

Figure 6.10 illustrates the relationship of the three levels, with data being gathered within the Configuration Management Database (CMDB), and feeding through the CMS into the Service Knowledge Management System and supporting the informed decision-making process.

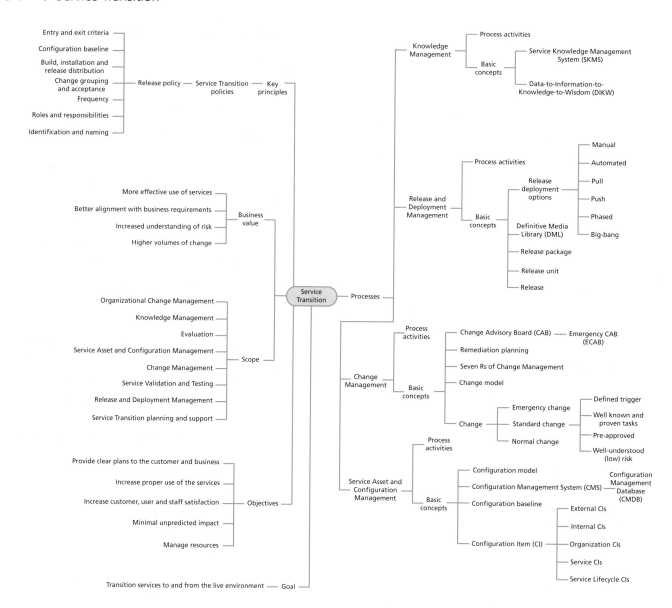

Figure 6.12 Overview of Chapter 6 (Service Transition)

The Knowledge Management process

The key activities within the Knowledge Management process (Figure 6.11) should include:

- **Defining a Knowledge Management strategy**   An overall strategy for Knowledge Management is required
- **Transferring knowledge**   Knowledge needs to be transferred to other parts of the organization at specific points in the lifecycle
- **Managing data and information**   Knowledge rests on the management of the information and data that underpins it
- **Using the Service Knowledge Management System**   Providing services to customers across time zones, work cycles and geographies requires good knowledge sharing across all locations and time periods of Service Operation.

6.6 SAMPLE QUESTIONS

1   Which statement about the relationship between the Configuration Management System (CMS) and the Service Knowledge Management System (SKMS) is correct?

   a   The SKMS is part of the CMS.

   b   The CMS forms part of the SKMS.

   c   The CMS and SKMS are the same thing.

   d   There is no relationship between the CMS and the SKMS.

2   Which of the following are examples of tools that might support the Service Transition phase of the Lifecycle?

   1   A tool to store definitive versions of software

   2   A workflow tool for managing changes

3   An automated software distribution tool

4   Testing and validation tools.

   a   1, 3 and 4 only

   b   1, 2 and 3 only

   c   All of the above

   d   2, 3 and 4 only.

3   The main goals of the Service Transition phase of the lifecycle are:

1   To enable the business change project or customer to integrate a release into their business processes and services

2   To reduce known errors and minimize the risks for services as they transition into production

3   To ensure that the services can be used in accordance with the requirements stated within the original service requirements

4   To provide the business with the details of the changing business processes, and carry out subsequent training of these business operational changes.

   a   1 and 4 only

   b   2 and 3 only

   c   1, 2 and 3 only

   d   All of the above.

4   It is critical that the Service Knowledge Management system contains a considerable quantity of data. What is the central repository of data called?

   a   The Configuration Management System

   b   The Definitive Media Library

   c The Service Level Agreement

   d The customers' self-service menu.

5   What is the BEST description of the Configuration Management System?

   a It holds appropriate details of all components of the IT infrastructure and the relationship between these components.

   b It represents any component that needs to be managed in order to deliver an IT service.

   c It represents the tools and databases that are used to manage an organization's knowledge and information throughout the whole of the Service Lifecycle.

   d It is a single repository holding details of the service model and the relationships between the different components of that service.

6   Which of the following is not an appropriate option for deploying a new service into production as described in the release and deployment process?

   a Big bang

   b Pilot

   c Phased

   d Pull.

Service Operation

7 Service Operation

Strategic objectives are ultimately realized through Service Operation, requiring effective and efficient delivery and support of services to ensure value for the customer and the service provider.

Time has passed and Brigitte is back at the alpine hotel again. Even though she thinks she travels too much, she likes to be back in the beautiful surroundings. She takes a quick walk around the hotel and notices that an expansion with a small water world is almost complete and that the construction of the conference facilities is progressing. She is amazed that the hotel staff are capable of managing two major projects while still running the hotel. After all, it is still the operation of the old part of the hotel that earns the money.

When the new conference services have been implemented, they will have to be operated according to the agreed service levels. Brigitte doesn't know much about hotel operation, but she imagines that it may include activities such as:

- Hosting and facilitation of conferences
- Monitoring and management of the air conditioning in the conference facilities
- Cleaning and maintenance of the conference facilities
- Measurement and reporting of the satisfaction of the conference delegates
- Training of new staff members.

7.1 GOALS AND OBJECTIVES

The main goal is to achieve effectiveness and efficiency in the delivery and support of services and to maintain stability while at the same time allowing for changes and improvement.

The main objectives of Service Operation are to:

- Deliver agreed levels of services to the business and customers
- Manage the applications, technology and infrastructure that support delivery of the services
- Support optimization of cost and quality.

7.2 SCOPE

Service Operation includes operation and management of:

- All aspects of the end-to-end services agreed with the business, including aspects done by third parties of the customers and end-users themselves
- Service Management processes that support the services
- Technology and infrastructure needed to deliver the services
- People who manage the technology, processes and services.

7.3 BUSINESS VALUE

Service Operation is the stage in the lifecycle where the plans, designs and optimizations are executed and measured. Service Operation is where actual value is seen by the business.

7.4 KEY PRINCIPLES

7.4.1 Communication

Effective communication in Service Operation ensures that all teams and departments are able to execute the standard activities involved in delivering services and managing the infrastructure. Issues can often be prevented or mitigated with appropriate communication.

Types of communication include:

- Routine operational communication
- Communication between shifts
- Performance reporting
- Communication in projects
- Communication related to changes
- Communication related to exceptions and emergencies
- Training of new or customized processes and Service Designs
- Communication of strategy and design to Service Operation teams.

There is no definitive medium for communication, nor is there a fixed location or frequency. In some organizations communication has to take place in meetings. Other organizations prefer to use e-mail or the communication inherent in their Service Management tools.

7.5 PROCESSES

The ITIL Foundation syllabus covers the following Service Operation processes:

- Event Management
- Incident Management
- Request Fulfilment
- Problem Management

- Access Management.

In addition the Service Operation book includes the Application Management, Technology Management and Operations Management activities, but as these are not part of the ITIL Foundation syllabus they will not be further discussed.

7.5.1 Event Management

During the next few years Brigitte regularly returns to the hotel. Actually, she went to the grand opening of the new conference centre. It started in the old reception where the hotel management proudly presented the control panel for the heating, sun panels and lights in the new conference centre.

Suddenly a beep sounded and a light on the control panel turned red. The shade of the face of the man who did the presentation soon reflected the colour of the lamp – he obviously didn't expect an alarm to go off in the middle of his presentation; but, on the other hand, it left him with the opportunity to show how advanced the system was. The beep, he explained, was an announcement from the system that a human intervention was required. In this case the temperature in the auditorium suddenly was unexpectedly low.

To come to this conclusion, the system had collected data from temperature sensors both inside the room and outside the building, as well as data from the heating equipment. The system then had correlated all the information, compared the result with the defined thresholds and determined to issue an alert.

7.5.1.1 Goals and objectives

- To provide a sound basis for operational monitoring and control
- To detect events, make sense of them, and determine the appropriate control action
- To act as a basis for automating routine operations management activities.

7.5.1.2 Basic concepts

Event

> **Definition**
>
> An **event** is a change of state which has significance for the management of the IT infrastructure or the delivery of an IT service.

Events are typically notifications created by a service, CI or monitoring tool.

Alert

> **Definition**
>
> An **alert** is a warning that a threshold has been reached, something has changed, or a failure has occurred.

Alerts are often created and managed by System Management tools and are managed by the Event Management process.

Event types

Types of event include the following:

- **Informational** – no action required; the event is logged. For example:
  - Notification that a scheduled workload has been completed
  - A user has logged in to an application
  - An e-mail has reached its recipient.

- **Warning** – typically generated when a threshold has been reached, enabling someone to react before things go wrong. Examples of this type of event are:
  - A server's memory utilization reaches within 5% of its highest acceptable performance level
  - The completion time of a transaction is 10% longer than normal.
- **Exception** – a service or device is operating abnormally and action is required:
  - A user attempting to log on to an application with an incorrect password
  - A device's Central Processing Unit performing above the acceptable utilization rate
  - A PC scan revealing the installation of unauthorized software.

7.5.2 Incident Management

On one of her recent trips, Brigitte one night got back to her room at the hotel to sleep. While brushing her teeth she noticed that the showerhead had fallen to the ground and was broken.

After finishing her tooth brushing she dialled the reception. The folder next to the telephone guided her on how to report an incident 'If you need any kind of assistance or want to report a problem, please call the reception by dialling 1'. The receptionist asked questions such as: 'What is your problem?', 'Is the shower completely useless or can you use it anyway?', 'Is it important to fix it now or can it wait till tomorrow?' and 'When do you plan to take a shower?'

Brigitte didn't need a shower at that moment – but she had to take one in the morning before going back to the factory at 8 a.m. The receptionist was unable to find someone who could fix the shower before 6 a.m. so he tried to identify a workaround: 'Brigitte, do you want to have another room (facing the street so it is a bit noisier) or have a key to the pool area and have your morning shower there?'

7.5.2.1 Goals and objectives

- To restore normal service as quickly as possible and to minimize the business impact of incidents
- To ensure that the best possible levels of service quality and availability are maintained.

7.5.2.2 Basic concepts

Incident and workaround

Definition

An **incident** is an unplanned interruption to a service or reduction in the quality of a service. Failure of a CI that has not yet impacted on service is also an incident.

In some cases it may be possible to find a workaround to an incident – a temporary way of overcoming the difficulties. But it is important that work on a permanent resolution continues where this is justified.

Definition

A **workaround** is a way of reducing or eliminating the impact of an incident or problem for which a full resolution is not yet available.

Examples would be restarting a failed Configuration Item (CI) or by making a manual amendment to an input file to allow a program to complete its run successfully.

Workarounds for problems (see below) are documented in known error records. Workarounds for incidents that do not have associated problem records are documented in the incident record.

Prioritization

An important aspect of logging every incident is to agree and allocate an appropriate priority – as this will determine how the incident is handled both by support tools and support staff. The priority is a category used to identify the relative importance of an incident.

The priority is based on the urgency of the incident (how quickly the business needs a resolution) and the level of impact it is causing.

An effective way of calculating these elements and deriving an overall priority level for each incident is shown in Figure 7.1.

An indication of impact is often the number of users being affected. However, in some cases the loss of service to a single user can have a major business impact so numbers alone are not enough to evaluate overall priority. Other factors that can also contribute to impact levels are:

- Risk to life or limb
- Number of services affected – may be multiple services
- Level of financial losses
- Effect on business reputation
- Regulatory or legislative breaches.

Timescales must be agreed for all incident handling stages depending on the priority of the incident

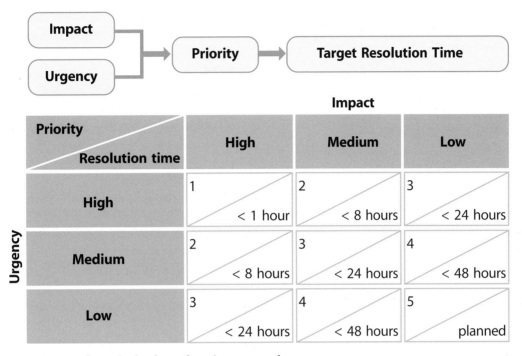

Figure 7.1 Calculating the priority based on impact and urgency

– based on the overall incident response and resolution targets within SLAs – and captured as targets within Operational Level Agreements (OLAs) and Underpinning Contracts. All support groups should be made fully aware of these timescales.

Major incident

A separate procedure, with shorter timescales and greater urgency, must be used for major incidents. A definition of what constitutes a major incident must be agreed and ideally mapped on to the overall incident prioritization system – such that it will be dealt with through the major incident process.

Where necessary, the major incident procedure should include the dynamic establishment of a separate major incident team under the direct leadership of the Incident Manager, formulated

to concentrate on this incident alone to ensure that adequate resources and focus are provided to finding a swift resolution.

Incident Model

Many incidents are not new. They involve dealing with something that has happened before and may well happen again. For this reason, some organizations find it helpful to predefine Incident Models.

> **Definition**
>
> An **Incident Model** is a way of predefining the steps that should be taken to handle a process for dealing with a particular type of incident in an agreed way.

The Incident Model should include:

- The steps that should be taken to handle the incident
- The chronological order these steps should be taken in, with any dependences or co-processing defined
- Responsibilities: who should do what
- Timescales and thresholds for completion of the actions
- Escalation procedures: who should be contacted and when
- Any necessary evidence-preservation activities.

7.5.2.3 Process activities

The key activities within the Incident Management process include (Figure 7.2):

- **Incident identification** Incidents may be detected by Event Management, by calls to the Service Desk, from web or other self-help interfaces, or directly by technical staff
- **Incident logging** All incidents must be logged and time-stamped, regardless of whether they are received through a Service Desk telephone call or whether automatically detected via an event alert. The log must include sufficient data to enable the incident to be managed
- **Incident categorization** Categories are used to identify the type of incident and to identify Service Requests so that they can be passed to the Request Fulfilment process
- **Incident prioritization** A priority is assigned based on impact and urgency. Priorities are dynamic and may be changed during the life of the incident
- **Initial diagnosis** If possible the incident should be resolved while the user is still on the phone. Sometimes the Service Desk analyst will

continue the work on the incident and contact the user when it has been resolved

- **Incident escalation**
  - **Functional escalation** The incident is transferred to a technical team with a higher level of expertise
  - **Hierarchic escalation** If incidents are of a serious nature, the appropriate managers must be notified – for informational purposes at least
- **Investigation and diagnosis** Each of the support groups involved with the incident handling will investigate and diagnose what has gone wrong
- **Resolution and recovery** When a potential resolution has been identified, this should be tested, applied and documented in the incident record
- **Incident closure** The Service Desk should check that the incident is fully resolved and that the users are satisfied and willing to agree the incident can be closed.

7.5.2.4 Relationships

The interfaces with Incident Management include:

- **Problem Management** Incident Management forms part of the overall process of dealing with problems in the organization. Incidents are often caused by underlying problems, which must be solved to prevent the incident from recurring. Incident Management provides a point where these are reported
- **Configuration Management** Provides the data used to identify and progress incidents
- **Change Management** Where a change is required to implement a workaround or resolution, this will need to be logged as an RFC and progressed through Change Management

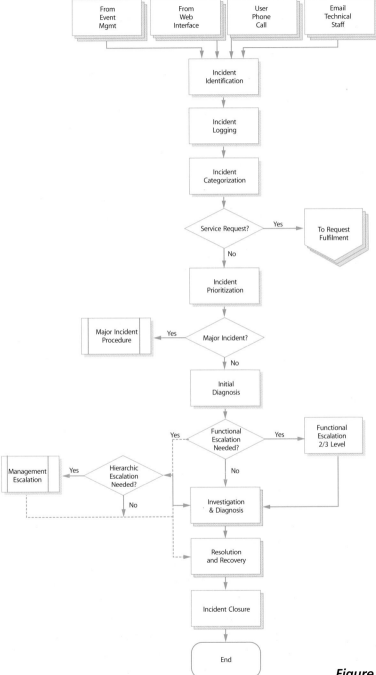

Figure 7.2 Incident Management process flow

- **Capacity Management** Incident Management provides a trigger for performance monitoring where there appears to be a performance problem
- **Availability Management** Will use Incident Management data to determine the availability of IT services and look at where the incident lifecycle can be improved
- **Service Level Management** The ability to resolve incidents in a specified time is a key part of delivering an agreed level of service.

7.5.3 Request Fulfilment

On another trip, Brigitte had forgotten her alarm clock so she needed to find another way to get a wake-up call. The hotel room contained an interactive television with a multitude of service menus. She turned on the television and went to the self-service menu (1. Wake up service, 2. Restaurant menu, 3. Reservation of restaurant tables, 4. Room service, 5. Opening hours in pool area etc.). She pressed '1' and '0630' to set the alarm for 6.30 a.m.

Brigitte reflected on the service system. It was quite smart – the guests were able to see most of the services provided and the system even handled a lot of them without human intervention.

7.5.3.1 Goals and objectives

- To provide a channel for users to request and receive standard services
- To provide information to users and customers about services and the procedure for obtaining them
- To source and deliver the components of requested standard services.

7.5.3.2 Basic concepts

Service Request

> **Definition**
>
> A **Service Request** is a request from a user for information, or advice, or for a standard change or for access to a service.

The term Service Request is used as a generic description for the many varying types of demand that are placed on the IT department by users. Many of these are actually small changes – low risk, frequently occurring, low cost etc. (e.g. a request to change a password, a request to install an additional software application onto a particular workstation, a request to relocate some items of desktop equipment) – or they may be just a question requesting information.

Request models

Many Service Requests will recur frequently, so a predefined request model can be devised to include the stages needed to fulfil the request, the individuals or support groups involved, target timescales and escalation paths.

The need for a request model can often be satisfied by implementing a standard change. The ownership of Service Requests resides with the Service Desk, which monitors, escalates, dispatches and often fulfils the user's request.

7.5.4 Problem Management

One time when Brigitte visited the hotel, the showerhead had been broken; as a result she had had to go to the pool area to have her morning shower. Because of this, the first thing Brigitte did when she arrived at the hotel room next time was to check if the shower was OK.

Not only was it OK but also a strap had been mounted on the showerhead to prevent it from falling to the floor if dropped.

Brigitte had not been the only one with a showerhead problem; a number of incidents had been reported, and an analysis was performed to identify the root causes of the problem. It turned out that the root causes were weaknesses in the showerheads combined with human behaviour. A number of solutions were examined before the problem was fixed, including replacement of all showerheads and mounting of a strap that prevents the showerheads from falling.

7.5.4.1 Goals and objectives

- To prevent incidents and resulting problems from happening, and to eliminate recurring incidents
- To minimize the impact of incidents that cannot be prevented.

7.5.4.2 Basic concepts

Problem, known error and resolution

Definition

A **problem** is the unknown cause of one or more incidents.

The cause is not usually known at the time a problem record is created, and the Problem Management process is responsible for further investigation.

Definition

A **known error** is a problem that has a documented root cause and a workaround.

As soon as the diagnosis is complete, and particularly where a workaround has been found, a known error record must be raised and placed in the known error database (KEDB), so that if further incidents or problems arise they can be identified and the service restored more quickly.

However, in some cases it may be advantageous to raise a known error record even earlier in the overall process, for example just for information purposes, even though the diagnosis may not be complete or a workaround found. So it is inadvisable to set a concrete procedural point exactly when a known error record must be raised. It should be done as soon as it becomes useful to do so.

Definition

A **resolution** is an action taken to repair the root cause of an incident or problem, or to implement a workaround.

Ideally, as soon as a solution has been found it should be applied to resolve the problem. However, in reality safeguards may be needed to ensure that this does not cause other difficulties.

If any change in functionality is required, this will require a Request for Change (RFC) to be raised and approved before the resolution can be applied.

Known error database

To allow quicker diagnosis and resolution of incidents and problems, previous knowledge of how they were overcome should be stored in a known error database (KEDB).

The known error record should hold exact details of the fault and the symptoms that occurred, together with precise details of any workaround or resolution action that can be taken to restore the service and resolve the problem.

The KEDB, like the Configuration Management System (CMS), forms part of the larger Service Knowledge Management System (SKMS).

Problem Model

Many problems will be unique and will require handling in an individual way. However, it is conceivable that some incidents may recur because of dormant or underlying problems.

Besides the creation of a known error record in the known error database to ensure quicker diagnosis, the creation of a Problem Model for handling such problems in the future may be helpful.

7.5.4.3 Process activities

Problem Management consists of two major processes:

- Reactive Problem Management, which is generally executed as part of Service Operation
- Proactive Problem Management, which is initiated in Service Operation, but generally driven as part of Continual Service Improvement.

The reactive Problem Management process is shown in Figure 7.3. This is a simplified chart to show the normal process flow, but in reality some of the states may be iterative or variations may have to be made in order to handle particular situations.

The key activities within the reactive Problem Management process include:

- **Problem detection** There are many ways a problem could be detected, including:
  - When an incident is reported to the Service Desk and the cause of it is unknown, even if the incident itself may be resolved by applying a workaround
  - When a technical support group identifies that a problem exists
  - When monitoring tools detect an infrastructure failure, which could lead to both an incident and a problem being identified
  - Through proactive Problem Management
- **Problem logging** All problems must be logged, and problem records must include all the details needed to manage the problem through its lifecycle, including links to related incidents
- **Problem categorization** Problems are categorized to enable analysis and reporting. It is advisable to use the same coding system as for incidents
- **Problem prioritization** Problems should be prioritized in the same way and for the same reason as incidents. Problem priority should take into account the frequency and impact of related incidents. Problem priority is also based on the severity of the problem, which is a measure of how serious the problem is from an infrastructure perspective, e.g. how long it will take to fix, or how much it will cost
- **Problem investigation and diagnosis** An investigation diagnoses the root cause of the problem. The speed and nature of the investigation, and the resources invested, should depend on impact, severity and urgency of the problem
- **Workarounds** A workaround is a way of reducing or eliminating the impact of a

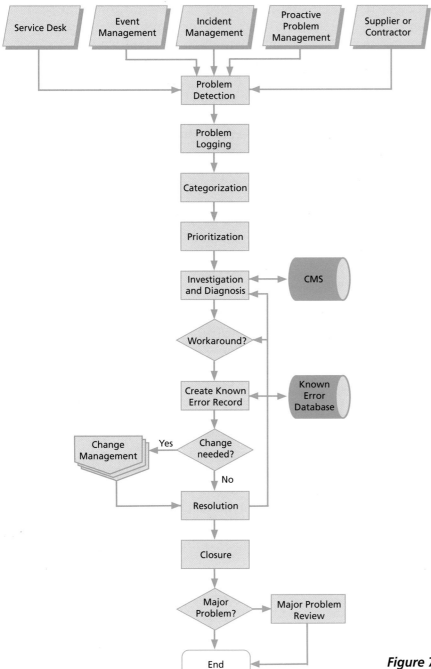

Figure 7.3 Reactive Problem Management process flow

problem, but not fully resolving its cause. If a workaround has been implemented, the problem record should remain open until the problem has been resolved

- **Raising a known error record** When diagnosis is complete, and particularly when a workaround has been found, a known error record should be raised and stored in the known error database (KEDB) so that further incidents or problems can be identified and the service restored more quickly. Sometimes it may be advantageous to raise a known error record earlier in the overall process

- **Problem resolution** Full resolution of a problem usually involves raising a Change Request. If the problem is very serious, this may be an Emergency Change Request. Sometimes it may not be possible to justify the change in a business case, and a decision may be made to leave the problem record open and rely on the workaround in the known error record

- **Problem closure** When the problem has been resolved, the problem record and related incident records should be closed. The record should be checked to ensure that it contains all required information and the status of related known error records should be updated

- **Major Problem Review** A review of every major problem should be conducted to learn lessons for the future. Major problem is defined by the priority system.

7.5.4.4 Relationships

The interfaces with Problem Management include:

- **Incident Management** Incident Management forms part of the overall process of dealing with problems in the organization. Incidents are often caused by underlying problems, which must be solved to prevent the incident from recurring. Incident Management provides a point where these are reported

- **Change Management** Problem Management ensures that all resolutions or workarounds that require a change to a Configuration Item (CI) are submitted through Change Management

- **Configuration Management** Problem Management uses the Configuration Management System (CMS) to identify faulty CIs and also to determine the impact of problems and resolutions

- **Release and Deployment Management** Is responsible for rolling problem fixes out into the live environment

- **Availability Management** Is involved with determining how to reduce downtime and increase uptime

- **Capacity Management** Some problems will require investigation by Capacity Management teams and techniques, e.g. performance issues

- **IT Service Continuity** Problem Management acts as an entry point into IT Service Continuity Management where a significant problem is not resolved before it starts to have a major impact on the business

- **Service Level Management** The occurrence of incidents and problems affects the level of service delivery measured by Service Level Management.

7.5.5 Access Management

Brigitte recalls the stay where the showerhead broke. She was not able to use the shower in her room but had to use the showers in the pool area. But the pool area was usually closed at the time when Brigitte needed to shower.

Therefore the receptionist helped her with getting access to the area:

- She checked the (security) policy to see if she was allowed to give a guest access to the pool area outside normal openings hours
- Then she identified Brigitte's card key in the hotel's database
- With that information she used the card key system to grant Brigitte the rights to enter the pool area outside normal opening hours
- And finally she filed a note about what she had done to ensure that Brigitte's card key rights would be returned to normal when the showerhead was fixed.

7.5.5.1 Goals and objectives

- To provide the right for users to be able to use a service or group of services
- To execute policies and actions defined in Security and Availability Management.

7.5.5.2 Basic concepts

Access, identity and rights

Access Management is the process that enables users to use the services that are documented in the Service Catalogue. It comprises the following basic concepts.

> **Definition**
>
> **Access** refers to the level and extent of a service's functionality or data that a user is entitled to use.

> **Definition**
>
> **Identity** refers to a unique name that is used to identify a user, person or role. The identity is used to grant rights to that user, person or role.

> **Definition**
>
> **Rights** (also called privileges) are the settings that enable a user to access a service or group of services.

Typical rights, or levels of access, are: read, write, execute, change and delete.

Services or service groups

Most users do not use only one service, and users performing a similar set of activities will use a similar set of services. Instead of providing access to each service for each user separately, it is more efficient to be able to grant each user – or group of users – access to the whole set of services that they are entitled to use at the same time.

Directory services

Directory services refers to a specific type of tool and database that is used to manage access and rights.

7.6 FUNCTIONS

7.6.1 Service Desk

7.6.1.1 Role

A Service Desk is a functional unit made up of a dedicated number of staff responsible for dealing with a variety of service incidents and events, often reported via telephone calls or web interfaces, or automatically reported via infrastructure events.

The Service Desk provides a single point of contact for all users. A good Service Desk can compensate for deficiencies elsewhere in the IT organization, but an ineffective Service Desk can give a poor impression of an otherwise very effective IT organization.

7.6.1.2 Objectives

The primary objective of the Service Desk is to restore the 'normal service' to users as quickly as possible. This may involve fixing a technical fault, fulfilling a Service Request or answering a query – anything that is needed to allow users to return to normal working.

Specific responsibilities of the Service Desk are:

- Logging all relevant incidents and Service Requests, categorizing and prioritizing them
- First-line investigation and diagnosis
- Resolving the incidents and Service Requests they are able to
- Escalating the incidents and Service Requests that they cannot resolve within agreed timescales
- Keeping users informed of progress
- Closing all resolved incidents, Service Requests and other calls
- Conducting customer/user satisfaction call-backs/surveys.

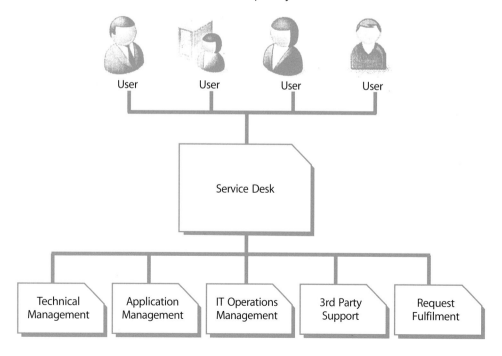

Figure 7.4   Local Service Desk

7.6.1.3 Organizational structures

There are many ways of structuring and locating Service Desks. The main options are:

- Local Service Desk
- Centralized Service Desk
- Virtual Service Desk
- Follow-the-sun.

In reality, an organization may need to implement a structure that combines a number of these options to meet the business needs fully.

Local Service Desk

This is where a Service Desk is co-located within or physically close to the user community it serves (Figure 7.4).

A local Service Desk often aids communication and gives a clearly visible presence, and can support local language and cultural differences. However, it can often be inefficient and expensive to resource as the volume and arrival rate of calls may not justify the minimum staffing levels required.

Centralized Service Desk

It is possible to reduce the number of Service Desks by merging them into a single location or a smaller number of locations by drawing the staff into one or more centralized Service Desk structures (Figure 7.5).

Centralized Service Desks can be more efficient and cost-effective, allowing fewer overall staff to deal with a higher volume of calls. It might still be necessary to maintain some 'local presence', but such staff can be controlled and deployed from the central desk.

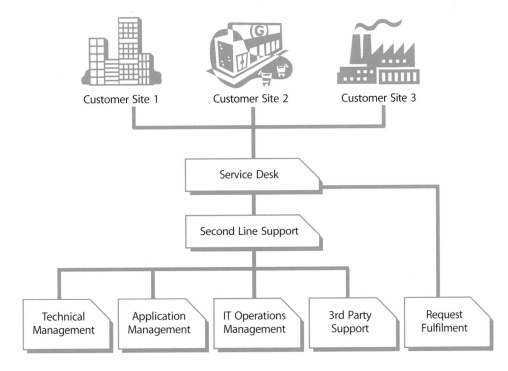

Figure 7.5 Centralized Service Desk

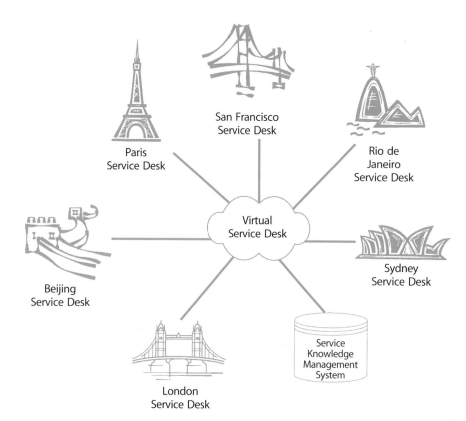

Figure 7.6   Virtual Service Desk

Virtual Service Desk

Through the use of technology and corporate support tools, it is possible to give the impression of a single, centralized Service Desk when, in fact, the personnel may be in any number or types of locations (Figure 7.6).

Virtual Service Desks bring in the option of 'home working', secondary support group, off-shoring or outsourcing, or any combination necessary to meet user demand.

Follow-the-sun

Some global organizations may wish to combine two or more of their geographically dispersed Service Desks to provide a 24-hour follow-the-sun

service. For example, a Service Desk in Asia Pacific may handle calls during its standard office hours, and at the end of this period staff may hand over responsibility for any open incidents to a European-based Service Desk. This kind of arrangement can give 24-hour coverage at relatively low cost as no desk has to work more than a single shift. However, common processes, tools, a shared database of information and robust handover procedures are needed for this to be successful.

7.6.2 Technical Management

7.6.2.1 Role

Technical Management refers to the people who provide technical expertise and management of the IT infrastructure. Technical Management plays a dual role:

- It is the custodian of technical knowledge and expertise related to managing the IT infrastructure. In this role Technical Management ensures that the knowledge required to design, test, manage and improve IT services is identified, developed and refined
- It provides the actual resources to support the Service Lifecycle. In this role Technical Management ensures that resources are effectively trained and deployed to design, build, transition, operate and improve the technology required to deliver and support IT services.

7.6.2.2 Objectives

The objectives of Technical Management are to help plan, implement and maintain a stable technical infrastructure to support the organization's business processes through:

- Well-designed and highly resilient, cost-effective technical topology
- Use of adequate technical skills to maintain the technical infrastructure in optimum condition
- Swift use of technical skills to speedily diagnose and resolve any technical failures that occur.

7.6.2.3 Overlap

The Technical Management function may overlap the IT Operations Management function because both functions play a role in management and maintenance of the IT infrastructure.

The Technical Management function may also overlap the Application Management function because both functions play an important role in the design, testing and improvement of

Configuration Items (CIs) that form part of IT services.

7.6.3 IT Operations Management

7.6.3.1 Role

IT Operations Management is responsible for performing the day-to-day operational activities required to manage and maintain the IT infrastructure and deliver the agreed level of IT services to the business.

The role of IT Operations Management is to execute the ongoing activities and procedures required to manage and maintain the IT infrastructure. These activities include:

- **Operations Control** Oversees the execution and monitoring of the operational activities and events in the IT infrastructure. In addition, Operations Control also performs the following specific tasks:
  - Console management
  - Job scheduling
  - Backup and restore
  - Print and output management
  - Maintenance activities
- **Facilities Management** The management of the physical IT environment, typically a data centre or computer rooms and recovery sites together with the power and cooling equipment.

As with many IT Service Management processes and functions, IT Operations Management has a dual role:

- It is responsible for executing the activities and performance standards defined during Service Design and tested during Service Transition

- At the same time it is part of the process of adding value to the different lines of business and to support the value network.

7.6.3.2 Objectives

- Achieving stability of an organization's day-to-day processes and activities
- Continual improvement to achieve improved service at reduced costs, while maintaining stability
- Swift application of operational skills to diagnose and resolve any IT Operations failures that occur.

7.6.3.3 Overlap

The IT Operations Management function may overlap the Technical Management function because both functions have a role in management and maintenance of the IT infrastructure.

The IT Operations Management function may overlap the Application Management function because both functions have a role in application support.

7.6.4 Application Management

7.6.4.1 Role

Application Management is responsible for managing applications throughout their lifecycle. Application Management also plays an important role in the design, testing and improvement of applications that form part of IT services. Application Management may therefore be involved in development projects, but it is not usually the same as the Application Development teams. One of the key decisions it contributes to is the decision of whether to buy or build an application.

Application Management has a dual role:

- It is the custodian of technical knowledge and expertise related to managing applications. In this role Application Management, working together with Technical Management, ensures that the knowledge required to design, test, manage and improve IT services is identified, developed and refined
- It provides the actual resources to support the Service Lifecycle. In this role Application Management ensures that resources are effectively trained and deployed to design, build, transition, operate and improve the technology required to deliver and support IT services.

In addition to these two high-level roles, Application Management also performs the following two specific roles:

- It provides guidance to IT Operations about how best to carry out the ongoing operational management of applications
- It integrates the Application Management Lifecycle into the Service Lifecycle.

7.6.4.2 Objectives

The objectives of Application Management are to support the organization's business processes by helping to identify functional and manageability requirements for application software, and then to assist in the design and deployment of those applications and to provide ongoing support and improvement of those applications.

These objectives are achieved through:

- Applications that are well designed, resilient and cost-effective

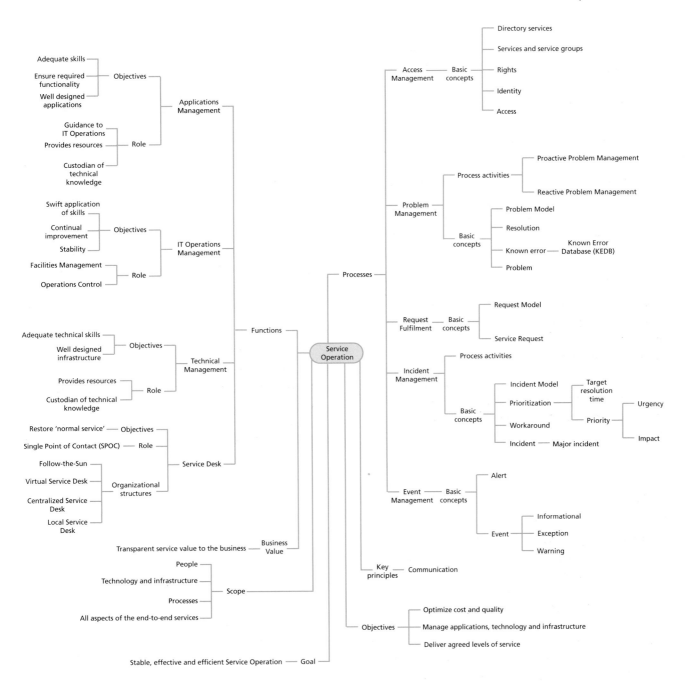

Figure 7.7 Overview of Chapter 7 (Service Operation)

- Ensuring that the required functionality is available to achieve the required business outcome
- Ensuring the organization of adequate technical skills to maintain operational applications in optimum condition
- Swift use of technical skills to speedily diagnose and resolve any technical failures that occur.

7.6.4.3 Overlap

The Application Management function may overlap the Technical Management function because both functions have an important role in the design, testing and improvement of Configuration Items (CIs) that form part of IT Services.

The Application Management function may overlap the IT Operations Management function because both functions have a role in application support.

7.7 SAMPLE QUESTIONS

1   Which of the following basic concepts are included in Access Management?

   1   Verifying the identity of users requesting access to services

   2   Setting the rights or privileges of systems to allow access to authorized users

   3   Defining security policies for system access

   4   Monitoring the availability of systems that users should have access to.

     a   2 and 4 only

     b   1 and 3 only

     c   2 and 3 only

     d   1 and 2 only.

2   Operations Control refers to:

   a   The managers of the Technical and Application Management functions

   b   Overseeing the execution and monitoring of operational activities and events

   c   The tools used to monitor and display the status of the IT infrastructure and applications

   d   The situation where the Service Desk is required to monitor the status of the infrastructure when operators are not available.

3   Which of the following statements about the Service Desk are correct?

   1   The Service Desk is a function that provides a means of communication between IT and its users for all operational issues

   2   The Service Desk is always the owner of the Incident Management process.

     a   2 only

     b   1 only

     c   Both of the above

     d   Neither of the above.

4   What is the PRIMARY objective of Service Operation?

   a   To ensure that the services are designed to meet the stated business objectives and that the four Ps have been considered

   b   To ensure that the service can be used in accordance with the requirements and constraints specified within the service requirements c To carry out activities and processes required to deliver and manage services at agreed levels

d To manage the technology that is used to deliver and support the services.

5 Which roles within the organization will take responsibility for carrying out the activities within the Incident Management process?

1 The Incident Management Process Owner

2 The Service Desk

3 Technical Management

4 Application Management.

   a 1 only

   b 2 only

   c 2, 3 and 4 only

   d 1 and 2 only.

6 Which of the following is the MAIN objective for Problem Management?

a To understand the cause of one or more incidents

b To prevent incidents from happening and to eliminate recurring incidents

c To restore service as quickly as possible and minimize the adverse impact on business operations

d To allow the functional escalation of incidents to the appropriate second and third level support teams.

Continual Service Improvement

8

8   Continual Service Improvement

Continual Service Improvement is responsible for managing improvements to services and service assets. The performance of the service provider is continually measured and improvements are made to services, capabilities and resources in order to increase efficiency, effectiveness and cost-effectiveness.

On the desk in Brigitte's room the hotel staff always leave a guest satisfaction form. The form contains statements like 'The room is clean' and she is asked to state to what degree she agrees.

Brigitte is an auditor in the pharmaceutical industry, so for professional reasons she is a bit curious to get insight into the quality management practices of the hotel. Brigitte asks the receptionist at the front desk. Fortunately, as there are no other guests in the reception area there is time for a deeper conversation and the following points emerge:

- The hotel is working with formally defined processes and procedures. The processes ensure that the hotel meets (or exceeds) the quality expectations of the guests in an efficient manner
- To ensure that processes continually reflect the changing requirements from the guests and the hotel infrastructure, a quality management system has been established. This quality management system also aims at improving the effectiveness and efficiency of the processes

- The form that Brigitte has just filled in is part of that quality system. The purpose is to measure and, if needed, adjust the effectiveness of the processes. For example, the cleaning processes have just been improved due to general dissatisfaction with the cleaning standard. The forms have been handed out to the guests before and after the change, to measure and control that the cleaning quality develops satisfactorily
- After the forms have been collected they are analysed. The results are presented to the management, who decide whether anything has to be changed. The result related to cleaning is presented to the hotel cleaners; it is hoped that the opinion of the guests will convince them that the change in the way they are working was a good idea (there was some resistance when the process was changed).

The receptionist continues to explain that before the hotel launched its conference services she joined a meeting where staff discussed whether the quality management system was to be improved to support the new conference services. Among other issues they evaluated whether the system would be able to identify the needs for improvement activities such as:

- Enhancing the booking process
- Developing the training programme for new staff members
- Renovating conference facilities after a couple of years.

Because it turned out that the system at the time wasn't able to catch important future quality issues, the staff agreed to improve the quality management system before launching the conference services.

8.1 GOALS AND OBJECTIVES

The primary goal of Continual Service Improvement (CSI) is to continually align and realign services to the changing business needs by identifying and implementing improvements to services that support business processes.

The main objectives of CSI are to:

- Review, analyse and make recommendations on improvement opportunities in each lifecycle stage
- Review and analyse service-level achievement results
- Identify and implement individual activities to improve service quality and the efficiency and effectiveness of Service Management processes
- Improve cost-effectiveness of delivering services without sacrificing customer satisfaction
- Ensure applicable quality management methods are used to support continual improvement activities.

8.2 SCOPE

CSI addresses three main areas:

- The overall health of Service Management as a discipline
- The continual alignment of the portfolio of services with the current and future business needs

- The maturity of the enabling processes for each service in a continual Service Lifecycle model.

8.3 BUSINESS VALUE

The CSI stage in the Service Lifecycle provides value to business in the form of improved services and the business gains achieved through realization of these improvements.

8.4 KEY PRINCIPLES

8.4.1 Governance

8.4.1.1 Enterprise governance

Enterprise governance describes a framework that covers both the corporate governance and the business management aspects of an organization to balance conformance and conformance requirements. Enterprise governance considers the whole picture to ensure that strategic goals are aligned and good management is achieved.

8.4.1.2 Corporate governance

Corporate governance is about promoting corporate fairness, transparency and accountability. Achieving a panacea of good corporate governance linked strategically with performance metrics will enable companies to focus all their energies on the key drivers that move their business forward.

8.4.1.3 IT governance

Definition

IT governance is the responsibility of the Board of Directors and executive management. It is an integral part of enterprise governance and consists of the leadership and organizational structures and processes that ensure that the organization's IT sustains and extends the organization's strategy and objectives.

IT Governance Institute (2001)

IT governance touches nearly every area of CSI. On the one hand, IT must comply with new rules and legislation and continually demonstrate compliance through successful independent audits by external organizations. On the other hand, IT is increasingly being called upon to 'do more with less' and create additional value while maximizing the use of existing resources.

These pressures fit perfectly together with the basic premise of ITIL: IT is a service business. Existing internal IT organizations must transform themselves into effective and efficient service providers or they will cease to be relevant to the business and, soon after, cease to exist. This continual and unceasing drive towards greater business value with greater internal efficiency is at the heart of CSI.

8.4.2 Deming Cycle

W Edwards Deming is well known for proposing the Deming Cycle for quality improvement. The four key stages of the cycle are 'Plan, Do, Check, Act' (PDCA) (Figure 8.1). Our goal in using the Deming Cycle is steady, ongoing improvement. It is a fundamental tenet of CSI.

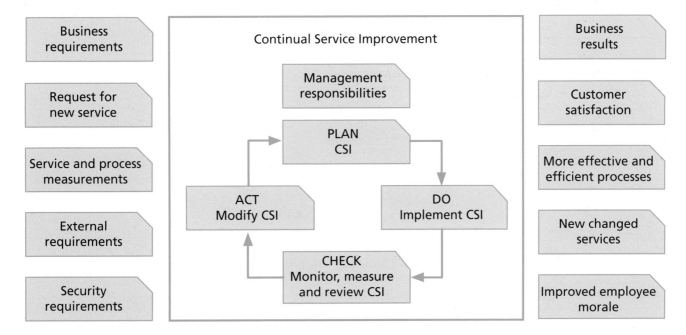

Figure 8.1 The Deming Cycle adapted for Continual Service Improvement

Planning for improvement initiatives (Plan)

At this stage goals and measures for success are established, a gap analysis is performed, action steps to close the gap are defined, and measures to ensure the gap was closed are established and implemented.

Implementation of improvement initiative (Do)

This includes development and implementation of a project to close the identified gaps, implementation of the improvement to Service Management processes, and establishment of the smooth operation of the process.

Monitor, measure and review services and Service Management processes (Check)

During this stage the implemented improvements are compared with the measures of success established in the Plan phase.

Continual Service and Service Management Process Improvement (Act)

This stage requires implementing the actual service and Service Management process improvements. A decision to keep the status quo, close the gap or add necessary resources needs to be made to determine whether further work is required to close remaining gaps and whether allocation of resources is necessary to support another round of

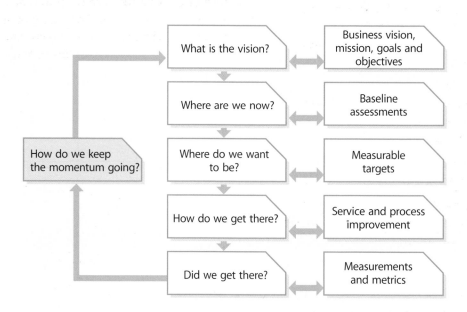

Figure 8.2 Continual Service Improvement model

improvement. Project decisions at this stage are the input for the next round of the PDCA cycle, closing the loop as input in the next Plan stage.

8.4.3 The Continual Service Improvement model

The CSI model (Figure 8.2) is an example of the Deming Cycle.

The model illustrates the constant cycle for improvement. The model consists of six steps:

1 Clarify the vision, taking into account business and IT vision, mission, goals and objectives

2 Assess the current situation to obtain an accurate, unbiased baseline of where the organization is right now

3 Determine the priorities for improvement, setting measurable targets. The full vision may be years away but this step provides specific goals and a manageable timeframe

4 Document an improvement plan to achieve higher-quality service provision by developing and implementing Service Management processes

5 Monitor achievements, making use of appropriate measurements and metrics

6 Maintain momentum by ensuring improvements are embedded and through continual re-evaluation.

8.4.4 Vision to measurements

A **vision** is a description of what an organization intends to become in the future (Figure 8.3).

The **mission statement** of an organization is a short but complete description of the overall purpose and intentions of that organization. It states what is to be achieved, but not how this should be done.

A **goal** is a means to help us to decide on a course of action.

The **objective** is the defined purpose or aim of a process, an activity or an organization as a whole. Objectives are usually expressed as measurable targets.

A **critical success factor** (CSF) is something that must happen if a process, project, plan or service is to succeed.

A **key performance indicator** (KPI) is a metric that is used to help manage a process, service or activity. Many metrics may be measured, but only the most important of these are defined as KPIs and used actively to manage and report on the process, service or activity. KPIs are used to measure the achievement of each CSF. For example, a CSF of 'protect IT services when making changes' could be measured by KPIs such as 'percentage reduction

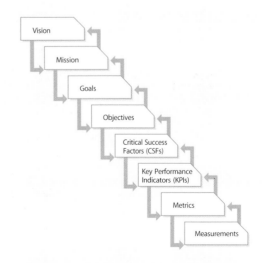

Figure 8.3 From vision to measurements

of unsuccessful changes', 'percentage reduction in changes causing incidents' etc.

It is recommended that in the early stages of a CSI programme only two to three KPIs for each CSF are defined, monitored and reported on. As the maturity of a service and Service Management processes increase, additional KPIs can be added. Based on what is important to the business and IT management, the KPIs may change over a period of time.

A **metric** is something that is measured and reported to help manage a process, service or activity. In general, a metric is a scale of measurement defined in terms of a standard, i.e. in terms of a well-defined unit.

8.4.5 Measurement

8.4.5.1 Why measure?

Monitoring and measuring is done (Figure 8.4) to:

- **Validate** To validate previous decisions

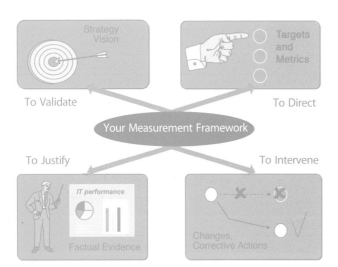

Figure 8.4 Why do we measure?

- **Direct** To set direction for activities in order to meet set targets
- **Justify** To justify, with factual evidence or proof, that a course of action is required
- **Intervene** To identify a point of intervention, including subsequent changes and corrective actions.

The four basic reasons to monitor and measure lead to three key questions:

- Why are we monitoring and measuring?
- When do we stop?
- Is anyone using the data?

Too often, we continue to measure long after the need has passed. Every time you produce a report you should ask: 'Do we still need this?'

When the hotel grew from a small family-run hotel to a larger hotel, the owner realized that he was losing his close relationship to all the hotel guests and employees, and he no longer knew enough about their needs and opinions to make the right decisions.

As a result the owner started to ask for facts like: 'I want a weekly report on the number of guests we have had and how many nights they stayed.' More and more reports were made until one day he realized that the hotel was spending a considerable amount of time making reports that were seldom or never used.

He decided to take a more structured approach to reporting:

- First he identified the ideal subjects to measure and report on. The list was quite long

■ Then he identified subjects to be measured from a practical point of view: what could be measured without too much work. Not all measurements were equally important. Some subjects required constant measuring, e.g. the number of guests/nights. Other subjects would be measured from time to time, for example the guest satisfaction with cleaning – this was measured before and after changes in the cleaning standard and in one week every year randomly chosen

■ Then it was just hard work, collecting the data, analysing it and acting on the outcome of the analysis

■ Once every six months the owner evaluates whether the most beneficial subjects are measured; if they are not, he sets up a new report and measurement requirement.

8.4.5.2 Baselines

An important starting point for highlighting improvement is to establish baselines as markers or starting points for later comparison. Baselines are also used to establish an initial data point to determine whether a service or process needs to be improved.

If a baseline is not initially established, the first measurement efforts will become the baseline. This is why it is essential to collect data at the outset, even if the integrity of the data is in question. It is better to have data to question than to have no data at all.

8.4.5.3 Types of metrics

It is important to remember that there are three types of metrics that an organization will need to collect to support CSI activities.

Technology metrics

These metrics are often associated with component-based and application-based metrics, such as performance, availability etc.

Process metrics

These metrics are captured in the form of critical success factors (CSFs), KPIs and activity metrics for the Service Management processes. These metrics can help determine the overall health of a process. Four key questions that KPIs can help answer are around quality, performance, value and compliance in following the process. CSI uses these metrics as input in identifying improvement opportunities for each process.

Service metrics

These metrics are the results of the end-to-end service. Component metrics can be used to compute the service metrics.

8.5 PROCESSES

The ITIL publication on CSI includes the seven-step improvement process as well as Service Measurement, Service Analysis, service reporting, Organizational Change Management and Communications Strategy and Planning activities.

None of these is part of the ITIL Foundation syllabus and they will not be further discussed here.

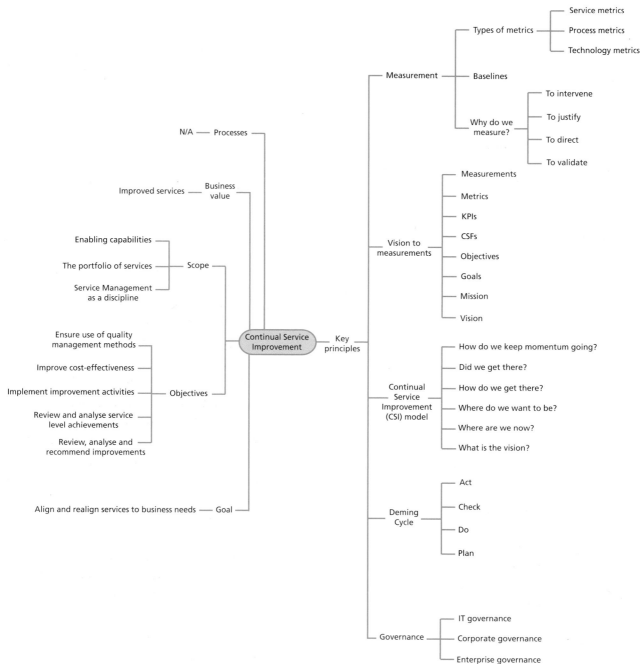

Figure 8.5 Overview of Chapter 8 (Continual Service Improvement)

8.6 SAMPLE QUESTIONS

1 Which statements about Key Performance Indicators (KPIs) and metrics are correct?

1 Service metrics measure the end-to-end service

2 KPIs should relate to a critical success factor

3 Continual Service Improvement (CSI) uses process metrics to identify improvement opportunities

4 KPIs can be both qualitative and quantitative.

a 1 only

b 2 and 3 only

c 1, 2 and 4 only

d All of the above.

2 What is contained within the 'Do' stage of the Deming cycle?

a A gap analysis is performed and the steps for closing the gaps are defined

b The actual implementation of the improvement initiative, and establishment of the smooth operation of the process

c Implementing the service or process improvements and establishing whether further work is necessary to close any remaining gaps

d Monitoring, measuring and reviewing the services and Service Management processes that were targeted for improvement.

3 Who should drive IT governance within an organization?

1 The Board of Directors and executive management of the organization

2 The customer

3 The Service Owners

4 The Service Desk.

a 1 only

b 2 only

c 2, 3 and 4 only

d All of the above.

4 In the Continual Service Improvement model, once all the measurements and metrics have been collated to confirm that the desired end result has been achieved, what activity should then take place?

a In order to close off the improvement activity, a confirmation of achievement of the business case should follow

b Capture the baseline assessments so that they can be used for later comparison

c Agree what needs to occur to ensure that the momentum for quality improvement is maintained

d Understand the high-level business objectives to ensure the vision has been captured.

5 Which of the following is NOT a type of metric that can be used to support Continual Service Improvement activities?

a Service metrics

b Technology metrics

c Process metrics

d Critical success factor (CSF) metrics.

Service Management
technology

9 Service Management technology

Technology has a major role in Service Management and this should be designed in, and mechanisms for maintaining and maximizing benefit from that technology must be in place.

The hotel has acquired and developed a number of tools and technologies to support its daily service processes:

- The bell
- Internet booking
- Asset register
- Invoicing system.

In addition it has systems that help staff monitoring and reporting on the performance of the hotel:

- Report on monthly occupancy rates
- Customer satisfaction survey system.

For the more physical management and control, the hotel has established monitoring and automation systems such as:

- Heat monitoring system
- Automated control of curtains due to sunshine
- Inter-TV system
- Video monitoring of luggage room
- Security log.

To support the development and management of new or changed services, the hotel has a tool for Release Management of the restaurant menu and a tool for Release Management of new work instructions. To make sure changes actually work, the hotel also has a tool for managing requirements and testing new equipment. Especially in the new conference centre, video equipment, wireless internet connection, pens and coffee machines have to be tested often.

9.1 USE OF TECHNOLOGY

Service Management is supported by technology in two ways:

- Enterprise-wide tools that support the broader systems and processes within Service Management
- Tools targeted more specifically at supporting a Service Lifecycle stage or parts of a stage.

Service Management technology enables the communication between service providers and customers. There are five modes in which technology interacts with a service provider's customers (Figure 9.1):

1 **Technology-free**   Technology is not involved in the service encounter

2 **Technology-assisted**   A service encounter in which only the service provider has access to the technology

3 **Technology-facilitated**   A service encounter in which both the service provider and the customer have access to the same technology

4 **Technology-mediated** A service encounter in which the service provider and the customer are not in physical proximity

5 **Technology-generated** A service encounter in which the service provider is represented entirely by technology, commonly known as self-service.

The tools and techniques are many and varied, including both proprietary and non-proprietary methods, and are beneficial in:

- Speeding up the Service Management processes
- Ensuring that standards and conventions are followed
- Offering prototyping, modelling and simulation facilities
- Enabling 'What if?' scenarios to be examined
- Enabling interfaces and dependencies to be checked and correlated.

9.2 SERVICE AUTOMATION

Automation should be considered to improve the utility and warranty of services.

9.2.1 Reasons for automation

Automation may offer advantages in many areas of opportunity, including the following:

- The capacity of automated resources can be more easily adjusted in response to variations in demand volumes
- Automated resources can handle capacity with fewer restrictions on time of access
- Automated systems present a good basis for measuring and improving service processes by holding constant the factor of human resources
- Many optimization problems, such as scheduling, routing and allocation of resources, require computing power that is beyond the capacity of human agents

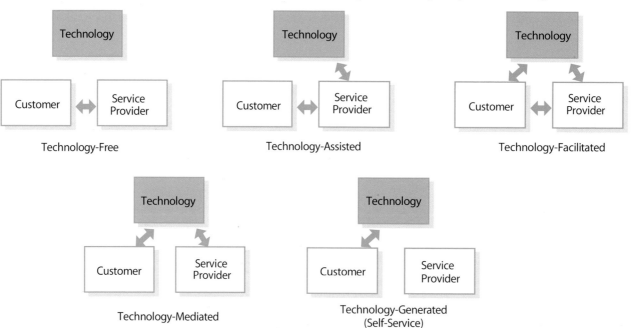

Figure 9.1 Types of service technology encounters

■ Automation is a means for capturing the knowledge required for a service process.

9.2.2 Preparing for automation

When automating, consider taking the following measures:

■ Simplify the service processes before automating them
■ Clarify the flow of activities, allocation of tasks, need for information, and interactions
■ In self-service situations, reduce the surface area of the contact users have with the underlying systems and processes
■ Do not be in a hurry to automate tasks and interactions that are neither simple nor routine.

9.3 SERVICE ANALYTICS

Information is static. It only becomes knowledge when placed in the context of patterns and their implications. Those patterns give a high level of predictability and reliability on how the data will change over time. By understanding patterns of information, we can answer 'How?' questions such as:

■ How does this incident affect the service?
■ How is the business impacted?
■ How do we respond?

This is service analytics.

Service analytics is useful to model existing infrastructure components and support services to the higher-level business services. Infrastructure events are then tied to corresponding business processes. The component-to-system-to-process linkage – also known as the service model – allows us to identify the business impact of an event clearly.

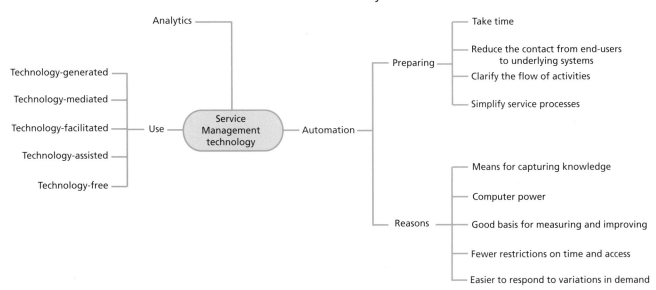

Figure 9.2 Overview of Chapter 9 (Service Management technology)

Instead of responding to discrete events, managers can characterize the behaviour of a service. This behaviour is then compared with a baseline of the normal behaviour for that time of day or business cycle.

With service analytics, not only can an operations group do a better job of identifying and correcting problems from the user's standpoint, but it can also predict the impact of changes to the environment. This same model can be turned around to show business demand for IT services. This is a high leverage point when building a dynamic provisioning or on-demand environment.

9.4 SAMPLE QUESTIONS

1 Which of the following areas would technology help to support in Service Transition?

1 An integrated Configuration Management System

2 A remote deployment tool

3 A workflow or process control engine to allow the predefinition and control of defined processes such as the change process model

4 A service-reporting tool to ensure that appropriate Service Level Agreements are demonstrated when a service is live in production.

a 1 and 2 only

b 1, 2 and 3 only

c 3 and 4 only

d All of the above.

2 Technology that is offered to the customer organization to facilitate their own capability is known as what?

a Discovery technology

b Remote control

c Self-help

d Diagnostic utilities.

How it all fits together

10

10 How it all fits together

Each lifecycle stage is dependent on input from and provides output to the other stages in the lifecycle. The primary connection point between each of the lifecycle stages is the Service Portfolio. It is the 'spine' which connects the stages to each other.

10.1 KEY LINKS, INPUTS AND OUTPUTS

The Service Portfolio acts as the connection point or the spine of the Service Lifecycle (Figure 10.1). It is the single integrated source of information on the status of each service, other service details, and

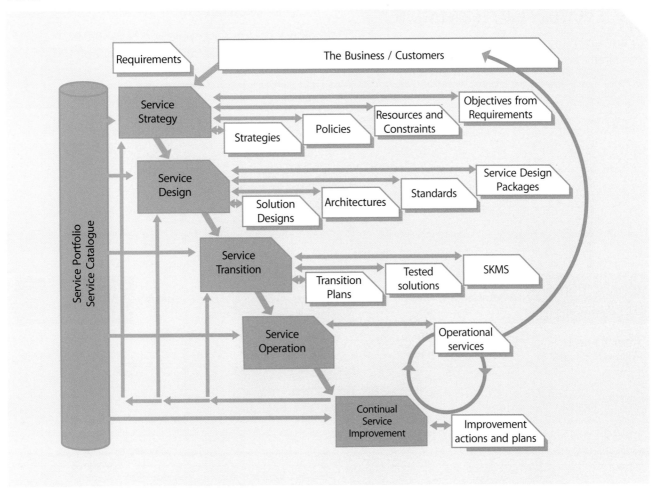

Figure 10.1 The Service Portfolio spine: key links, inputs and outputs in the Service Lifecycle

the interfaces and dependencies between services. The information within the Service Portfolio is used by the activities within each stage of the Service Lifecycle.

Figure 10.1 gives a good overview of the links, inputs and outputs involved at each stage of the Service Lifecycle. It illustrates the key outputs produced by each stage, which are used as inputs by the subsequent stages.

10.2 STRATEGY IMPLEMENTATION

For any given market space, Service Strategy defines the portfolio of services to be offered and the customers to be supported. This in turn determines the Service Portfolio that needs to be supported with design, transition and operation capabilities (Figure 10.2).

Lifecycle capabilities are defined in terms of the systems, processes, knowledge, skills and experience required at each stage to effectively support the Service Portfolios. Interactions between Service Management capabilities are clearly defined and managed for an integrated and systematic approach to Service Management.

Service Design and operation capabilities determine the type of transition capabilities

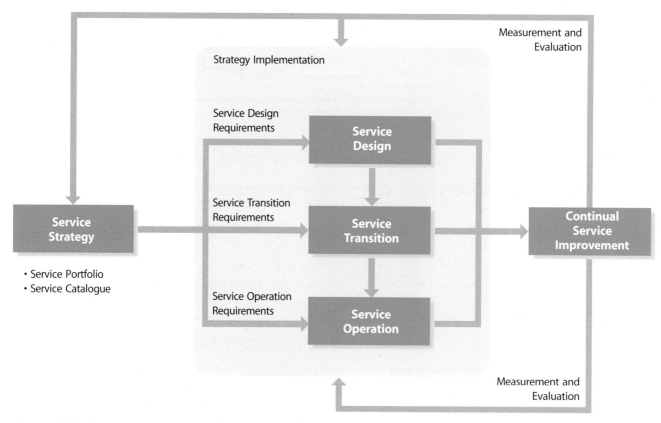

Figure 10.2 Strategy implementation through the Service Lifecycle

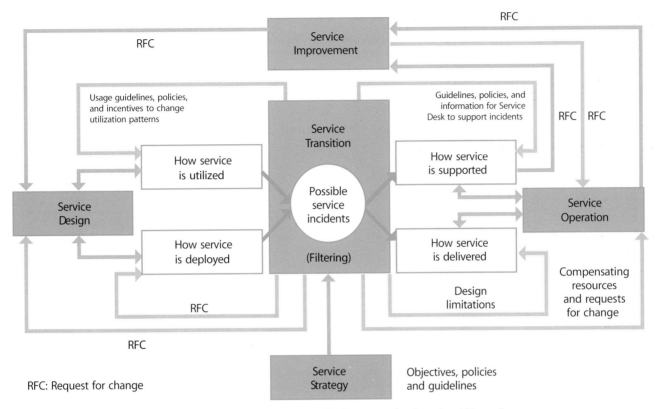

Figure 10.3 Service Management processes are applied across the Service Lifecycle

required. They determine the portfolio of Service Designs and the operating range of the service provider in terms of models and capacities. Strategies are ultimately realized through Service Operation.

Transition capabilities determine the costs and risks managed by a service provider. How quickly a service is transitioned from design to operations depends on the capabilities of the Service Transition stage. Service Transition provides the decision analysis necessary to analyse, evaluate and approve strategic initiatives. In this manner, transition capabilities act not only as filters but

also as amplifiers that increase the effectiveness of design and operation.

Service Strategy requires Continual Service Improvement (CSI) to drive feedback through the lifecycle elements to ensure that challenges and opportunities are not mismanaged.

10.3 SPECIALIZATION AND COORDINATION

Specialization and coordination are necessary in the lifecycle approach. Feedback and control between the functions and processes within and across the elements of the lifecycle make

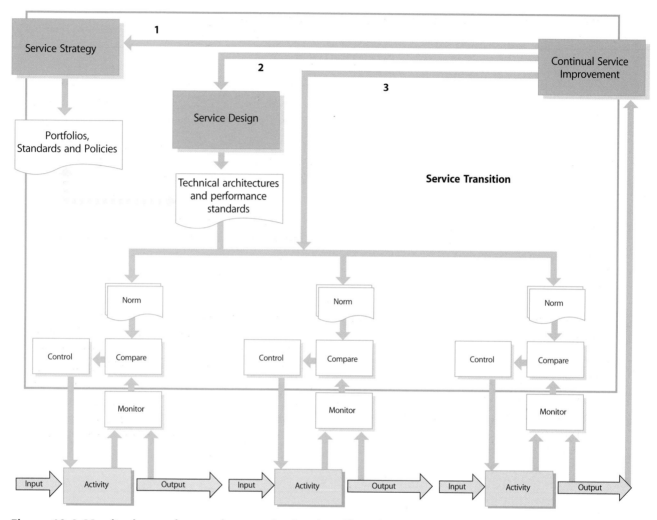

Figure 10.4 Monitoring and control across the Service Lifecycle

these possible. The dominant pattern in the lifecycle is the sequential progress starting from Service Strategy through to Service Delivery, Service Transition, Service Operation and CSI. That, however, is not the only pattern of action. Every element of the lifecycle provides points for feedback and control (Figure 10.3).

10.4 MONITORING AND CONTROL

Each activity in a Service Management process should be monitored. The role of operational monitoring and control is to ensure that the process or service functions exactly as specified, which is why they are primarily concerned with maintaining the status quo.

Figure 10.4 illustrates the monitoring and control of a process or of the components used to deliver a service.

The norms and monitoring and control mechanisms are defined in Service Design, but they are based on the standards and architectures defined during Service Strategy.

Notice that the second level of monitoring in this monitor control loop is performed by the CSI processes through Service Strategy and Service Design. These relationships are represented by the numbered arrows on the figure as follows:

1 In this case CSI has recognized that the service will be improved by making a change to the Service Strategy. This could be the result of the business needing a change to the Service Portfolio, or that the architecture does not deliver what was expected

2 In this case the Service Level Requirements (SLRs) need to be adjusted. It could be that the service is too expensive or because Operations Management is unable to maintain service quality in the current architecture

3 In this case the norms specified in Service Design are not being adhered to. This could be because they are not appropriate or executable, or because of a lack of education or communication. The norms and the lack of compliance need to be investigated and action taken to rectify the situation.

10.5 CONTINUAL SERVICE IMPROVEMENT

An organization can find improvement opportunities throughout the entire Service Lifecycle. Figure 10.5 shows the interaction that should take place between each lifecycle stage.

An IT organization does not need to wait until a service or Service Management process is transitioned into the operations area to begin identifying improvement opportunities.

CSI will make use of the methods and practices found in many ITIL processes such as Problem Management, Availability Management and Capacity Management used throughout the lifecycle.

The use of the outputs, in the form of flows, matrices, statistics or analysis reports, will provide valuable insight into the design and operation of services. This information, combined with new business requirements, technology specifications, capabilities, budgets, trends and possibly external legislative and regulatory requirements, will be vital to CSI to determine what needs to be improved.

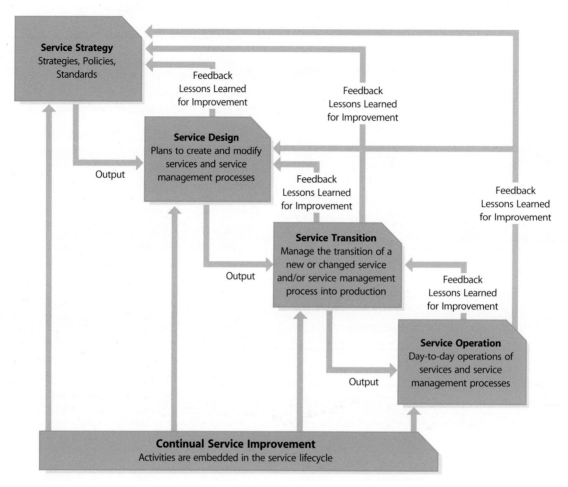

Figure 10.5 Continual Service Improvement throughout the Service Lifecycle

The examination and exam preparation

11　The examination and exam preparation

11.1　THE EXAMINATION

The examination is a closed-book paper consisting of 40 multiple-choice questions. All 40 questions should be attempted. Each question has four choices, and the candidate must select one of these to answer a question. Only one of the choices is correct.

The examination can be taken either on paper or online.

There is a maximum of 60 minutes to answer the paper. Candidates sitting the examination in a language other than their native language used in their business setting have a maximum of 75 minutes and are allowed to use a dictionary.

Candidates must answer 26 or more questions correctly to pass the examination, corresponding to a pass score of 65%.

Candidates who fail may retake the examination. There is no limit to the number of times a candidate may re-sit the examination.

11.2　EXAM PREPARATION

Attending an accredited Foundation training course is strongly recommended but not a prerequisite to sitting the examination. Candidates should note that the overall public examination pass rates are notably lower than the rates for candidates who have attended an accredited training course. Candidates are recommended to study for at least 18 hours prior to the exam.

You should start preparing for the examination from the first day of the course. Use an effective note-taking system, and review the course material regularly. Transfer information to be learned onto note cards and review them every day.

Homework and self-study will be expected. Make appointments with yourself (and your surroundings) for study time.

Practise taking the examination to help familiarize yourself with it. You can use the sample tests in this publication, and your training provider will also provide you with recent sample papers. Because the examination is a timed test, you should prepare for your upcoming test under similar conditions. Make sure that whenever you take practice tests, you time yourself using the same amount of allotted time that will be allowed on the real test. Know in advance how many minutes you can spend per question and every few questions check yourself against the clock to see how you are doing.

Prepare far enough in advance so that you can actually relax the night before the exam.

During the examination:

- Read each question carefully to make sure you understand the type of answer required
- Come up with the answer in your head before looking at the possible answers
- Read and consider all of the answer choices before you choose the one that best responds to the question

- Make sure you answer the question that is being asked
- There will be no trick questions so do not waste time and energy looking for catch questions
- Answer the easy questions first, then go back and answer the more difficult ones
- When attempting difficult questions, eliminate as many incorrect answers as you can, then make an educated guess from among those remaining
- Do not spend too much time on any one question
- Check that you have answered every question. Your scores on the multiple-choice tests are based on the number of questions you answer correctly. There is no penalty for guessing
- Review your work. If you finish a test before time is up, go back and check your work
- Do not keep on changing an answer – usually your first choice is the right one, unless you misread the question.

Sample ITIL version 3 Foundation Examination

12 Sample ITIL version 3 Foundation Examination

12.1 INSTRUCTIONS

All 40 questions should be attempted.

There are no trick questions.

You have 60 minutes to complete this paper. Candidates sitting the examination in a language other than their native language have a maximum of 75 minutes and are allowed the use of a dictionary.

You must get 26 or more answers correct to pass.

More sample papers will be provided by your course provider.

12.2 QUESTIONS

1   What is the primary objective of Financial Management?

   a   Calculating and assigning a monetary value to a service or service component

   b   To provide operational visibility and financial quantification of the value of the assets underlying the provisioning of services

   c   To provide justification that the utility and warranty have been delivered

   d   To avoid excess service capacity that would generate costs without adding value.

2   Which of these is NOT a value that Problem Management provides to the business:

   a   Higher availability of IT services

   b   Higher productivity of business and IT staff

   c   More closely aligned service levels to meet the business requirements

   d   Reduction in the cost of fire-fighting or resolving repeat incidents.

3   Which of the following is NOT an activity in the Service Level Management process?

   a   Monitor service performance against the Service Level Agreement (SLA) and produce service reports

   b   Conduct service review meetings and instigate service improvement

   c   Build a positive relationship with third-party suppliers to ensure that the end-to-end service is managed

   d   Determine, document and agree requirements for new services and compile the SLA.

4   Which are outputs of the Change Management process from the following four:

   1   An incident ticket

   2   Minutes of the CAB meeting

   3   The Change Schedule

   4   The Projected Service Outage Report.

      a   1 and 2 only

b 1, 3 and 4 only

c 2, 3 and 4 only

d All of the above.

5 What is the main activity associated with Demand Management?

a Developing the requirements for service utility

b Providing the appropriate value from the Service Level Package

c Understanding the value that IT needs to give to the business

d Understanding Patterns of Business Activity.

6 Which of the following are the main objectives for the Service Desk?

1 To provide management information

2 To restore normal service to the users as quickly as possible

3 To manage the incident through its lifecycle

4 To prevent problems and resulting incidents from happening.

a 1, 2 and 4 only

b 3 and 4 only

c 1, 2 and 3 only

d All of the above.

7 Who is accountable for a service across its complete lifecycle?

a The Service Desk

b The Service Level Manager

c The Service Owner

d The Process Owner.

8 Where within the Service Lifecycle do you confirm the service will meet the business requirements before deployment?

a Service Operation

b Service Transition

c Service Design

d Continual Service Improvement.

9 Which of the following statements BEST describes the difference between an Operational Level Agreement (OLA) and an Underpinning Contract (UC)?

a The OLA is an underpinning agreement with legally binding terms, whereas the UC supports the SLA and is therefore not formal.

b The OLA is an internal document that defines the working relationship between different groups within the service provider organization, whereas the UC is a legally binding document for a supplier in support of the SLA.

c The UC defines targets and responsibilities that are required to meet agreed Service Level Targets in a Service Level Agreement, whereas the OLA describes best endeavours for a service.

d There are no differences between an UC and an OLA as they both support the SLA.

10 There are five key aspects for a successful Service Design stage. Which aspect is missing from the list below?

1 The design of the Service Management systems and tools

2 The design of the technology architectures

3 The design of the processes

4 The design of the measurement methods and metrics.

   a The design of the Service Design Package (SDP)

   b The design of the documentation

   c The design of the service solution

   d The design of the business processes.

11 Which of the following is the CORRECT definition of a business case?

   a The decision support and planning tool to predict the costs associated with the implementation of a new service

   b A justification for a significant item of expenditure, which will include information about costs, benefits, options, risks and possible problems

   c The quantification of the costs of each service and how each service is consumed

   d The documentation that demonstrates the visibility and accountability of each business unit.

12 What is the associated activity within the 'Plan' stage of Deming's PDCA cycle for Continual Service Improvement?

   a Implement the improvement initiative

   b Monitor and measure the services

   c Establish goals and measurements for success, and perform gap analysis

   d Determine whether any further work is required.

13 Which of the following functions has a key objective to provide the technical expertise and specialized resources to the overall IT infrastructure, throughout the whole of the lifecycle?

   a Technical Management

   b IT Operations

   c Incident Management

   d Application Management.

14 Which of the following are recognized Service Desk types?

   1 A local Service Desk

   2 A central Service Desk

   3 An operations bridge Service Desk

   4 A virtual Service Desk.

   a 2 and 4 only

   b 1 and 3 only

   c 1, 2 and 4 only

   d All of the above.

15 Which of the following BEST describes the definition of reliability?

   a How easily a service or component can be fixed

   b The ability of an external supplier to meet the terms of their contract

   c Mean time to restore

   d The freedom from failure under agreed conditions.

16 In order to optimize the efficiency of the change process, many low-risk routine changes may be categorized as pre-authorized by Change Management. What type of change is this known as?

   a A Service Request

   b A change request

   c A normal change

   d A standard change.

17 What is contained within the Definitive Media Library?

   a Secure definitive authorized versions of both software and media CIs which have passed quality assurance checks

   b The relationship model of all service assets, infrastructure and individual components that make up a service

   c Secure definitive authorized versions of both software and media CIs which are waiting to pass quality assurance checks

   d Secure back-up tapes.

18 Which of the following is the CORRECT stage in the DIKW model where experiences, ideas, insights, values and judgements are applied?

   a Data

   b Information

   c Knowledge

   d Wisdom.

19 In a RACI authority matrix, the people who need to be kept up to date on the progress of an activity would have which description by their role?

   a Consult

   b Inform

   c Consider

   d Impacted.

20 The PRIMARY goal of Continual Service Improvement is BEST described as:

   a To continually align and re-align IT services to the changing business needs by identifying and implementing improvements to IT services that support business processes

   b To review, analyse and make recommendations on improvement opportunities across each lifecycle phase

   c To improve the cost-effectiveness of delivering IT services in order that the organization perceives that it is receiving good value for money

   d To design services that meet the original specifications and satisfy business objectives.

21 Which of the following are key elements that need to be defined as part of a process?

   1 The activities contained within the process

   2 The process policy

   3 Roles within the organization that will need to carry out the process

   4 Appropriate metrics for the process.

   a 1, 2 and 3 only

   b 3 and 4 only

   c 1, 2 and 4 only

   d All of the above.

22 Performance across Service Management can be significantly enhanced by the use of automation. Which of the following are appropriate options for automation?

1 Performance measurement

2 Automation of routine tasks such as the handling of Service Requests

3 Service reporting

4 Design and modelling.

    a 1 and 3 only

    b 1 and 2 only

    c 2, 3 and 4 only

    d All of the above.

23 Who is accountable for the release and deployment process?

    a The Deployment Manager

    b Members of the Application Management Function

    c The Service Desk

    d The Release and Deployment Process Owner.

24 Which of the following tasks would IT Operations NOT be responsible for?

    a Incident resolution

    b To manage applications throughout their lifecycle

    c Managing the facilities environment

    d Monitoring events.

25 During the Incident Management process, staff at the Service Desk are often unable to resolve the incident themselves so they would escalate the incident to a more technical team. What type of escalation is this known as?

    a Functional

    b Hierarchic

    c Problem Management

    d Call closure.

26 Which of the following statements BEST describes the key objective of Supplier Management?

    a To manage the internal teams to ensure that they deliver to their Operational Level Agreements

    b To manage suppliers and the services they supply to provide a quality service

    c To sit on the CAB on behalf of the supplier to represent a service

    d To record the list of preferred suppliers.

27 Which of the following are appropriate examples of a Service Request?

1 A password change or reset

2 A minor code change from a user to modify a particular application

3 The relocation of some desktop equipment

4 A question requesting information.

    a 1, 2 and 3 only

    b 2, and 4 only

    c 1, 3 and 4 only

    d All of the above.

28   In which function does Facilities Management sit?

   a   The Service Desk

   b   IT Operations

   c   Application Management

   d   Technical Management.

29   When is the BEST time for a Service Design Package (SDP) to be produced?

   a   During the Service Strategy stage each time a new service is added to the Service Portfolio

   b   During the Service Design stage each time a new service is added to the Service Catalogue

   c   During the Service Design stage as the final output leading into the Service Transition stage

   d   During the Service Transition stage as the final output leading into the Service Operation stage.

30   Which of the ITIL core best practices provides guidance on how to design, develop and implement Service Management as an organizational capability as well as a strategic asset?

   a   Service Strategy

   b   Service Design

   c   Service Transition

   d   Service Operation.

31   ITIL is BEST characterized as:

   a   An international standard

   b   A framework of good practice

   c   A certified world qualification scheme

   d   An international methodology.

32   Which of the following four options are suitable technology examples that would support efficiency and effectiveness in Service Operation?

   1   An automated call-distribution system for the Service Desk

   2   Customer self-help on the organization's intranet

   3   Remote control

   4   An integrated Service Management product.

      a   1, 3 and 4 only

      b   2 only

      c   1, 2 and 4 only

      d   All of the above.

33   Which of the following is the CORRECT sequence of activities during the incident lifecycle after the incident has been identified?

   a   1 – Initial diagnosis and possible escalation. 2 – Incident categorization. 3 – Incident logging. 4 – Incident prioritization. 5 – Investigation and diagnosis. 6 – Incident closure. 7 – Resolution and recovery.

   b   1 – Incident logging. 2 – Incident prioritization. 3 – Initial diagnosis and possible escalation. 4 – Investigation and diagnosis. 5 – Resolution and recovery. 6 – Incident categorization. 7 – Incident closure.

c   1 – Incident categorization. 2 – Incident logging. 3 – Incident prioritization. 4 – Initial diagnosis and possible escalation. 5 – Investigation and diagnosis. 6 – Resolution and recovery. 7 – Incident closure.

d   1 – Incident logging. 2 – Incident categorization. 3 – Incident prioritization. 4 – Initial diagnosis and possible escalation. 5 – Investigation and diagnosis. 6 – Resolution and recovery. 7 – Incident closure.

34   Which of the following processes would need to formally review risk?

a   Information Security, IT Service Continuity and Change Management

b   Service Catalogue Management, Supplier Management and Financial Management

c   Incident, Problem and Event Management

d   Service Design and Service Transition.

35   Which of the following is the PRIMARY objective of Access Management?

a   To provide the right for users to be able to use a service at all times to support their business processes

b   To align IT security with business security and ensure it is effectively managed

c   To provide the right for users to be able to use a service or group of services through the execution of the policies defined in Security and Availability Management

d   To ensure that IT services can be resumed in the event of a disaster, within required and agreed business timescales.

36   To answer the question 'Where are we now?' in the Continual Service Improvement model, we need to know:

a   How we will keep the momentum going

b   The current baseline assessments

c   The business vision

d   The new measurement targets.

37   Good Service Design is dependent on the effective and efficient use of the four Ps – People, Processes, Products and:

a   Plans

b   Partners

c   Procedures

d   Policies.

38   Which of the Service Operation functions would decide to buy off-the-shelf software packages to support the business processes?

a   The Service Desk

b   Technical Management

c   Application Management

d   IT Operations.

39   Which of the following statements is the correct definition for utility?

a   Perception by the customer of the positive attributes of a service

b   Perception by the customer of the positive performance of a service

c   The service is fit for use

d   The delivery of value creation to customers.

40   Within which lifecycle stage is the Service
      Portfolio determined?

      a   Service Strategy

      b   Service Design

      c   Service Transition

      d   Service Operation.

Answers 13

13 Answers

CHAPTER 2 (INTRODUCTION TO SERVICE MANAGEMENT)

1 d – Syllabus ref: 03-01

2 b – Option (c) and option (d) describe a process characteristic. Option (a) partially describes a function but it would not just cover a single task (2.2.2 definition of a function: a team or group of people and the tools they use to carry out one or more processes or activities)

3 c – RACI is an acronym for 'Responsible-Accountable-Consulted-Informed' (2.2.3.2)

4 c – Except for option 2, which is the responsibility of the Service Owner or the Service Level Manager, the rest of the activities form part of the responsibilities of the Process Owner (2.2.4)

5 b – Option (a) describes the roles within Service Operation, option (c) misses components related to external suppliers, and option (d) describes a responsibility of the Service Level Manager (2.2.5 definition: a role that is accountable for the delivery of a specific service).

CHAPTER 4 (SERVICE STRATEGY)

1 a – The Service Design Package is an output from Service Design (4.1, 4.2)

2 c – Option (a) refers only to warranty, option (b) describes just the list of the services, and option (d) refers to utility (4.3.1)

3 d – Options (a), (b) and (c) contain only component parts of the Service Portfolio (4.4.2 definition: the complete set of services that are managed by a service provider)

4 c – NOT option 4, as this would be done following the business case being approved (4.4.3 and Table 4.1; definition: justification for a significant item of expenditure).

CHAPTER 5 (SERVICE DESIGN)

1 d – Syllabus ref: 04-03

2 a – Syllabus ref: 05-44

3 a – Syllabus ref: 05-45

4 b – The organizational structure would be decided during the Service Strategy stage (5.1)

5 b – Option (a) is incorrect as this describes a service provider, option (c) is the definition of an OLA, and option (d), although nearly correct, does not state that the responsibilities of the customer are included in the SLA (5.5.2.2 definition of SLA: an agreement between an IT service provider and a customer).

CHAPTER 6 (SERVICE TRANSITION)

1 b – Syllabus Ref: 03-16

2 c – Syllabus Ref: 08-02

3 c – Option 4 would be carried out by the business itself as IT would only be indirectly

involved with the training activities for the actual business operational change (6.1)

4 a – Option (b) describes the Definitive Media Library where copies of software and media are stored; in option (c) the SLA would hold some data, but all pertaining to the service only; and in option (d) the customers' self-service menu shows the customers what services they can obtain (6.5.1.2 and Figure 6.3)

5 a – Option (b) is describing a Configuration Item, option (c) describes the SKMS and although option (d) is partially accurate, the CMS does not have to be a single repository (6.5.1.2 definition for CMS: a set of tools and databases that are used to manage an IT service provider's configuration data)

6 b – A pilot is describing the state of a new IT service once it has first been deployed and before mass roll-out (6.5.3.2).

CHAPTER 7 (SERVICE OPERATION)

1 d – Syllabus Ref: 05-83

2 b – Syllabus Ref: 06-02

3 b – Syllabus Ref: 06-01

4 c – Option (a) is an objective of Service Design, option (b) is an objective of Service Transition and option (d) is a small part of the coverage of Service Operation (7.1)

5 c – In option (a) the Process Owner is accountable for the process, and in option (b) the Service Desk is responsible for the incident through its lifecycle but all teams will have to take responsibility for the process if they are dealing with incidents (7.5.2.2, 7.6.1.1)

6 b – Option (a) describes an activity within Problem Management, option (c) is an objective of Incident Management and option (d) describes the incident functional escalation process (7.5.4.1).

CHAPTER 8 (CONTINUAL SERVICE IMPROVEMENT)

1 d – Syllabus Ref: 04-10

2 b – Option (a) describes the Plan stage, option (c) describes the Act stage and option (d) describes the activities in the Check stage (8.4.2)

3 a – It is only members of the Board of Directors and executive management who should drive IT governance, although all the other roles may have a part to play in feedback or following the processes (8.4.1 definition of IT governance: ensuring that policies and strategy are actually implemented, and that required processes are correctly followed)

4 c – This describes the concept of 'How to keep the momentum going'. Option (a) would have taken place during the 'Did we get there?' stage, option (b) describes the data requirements at the 'Where are we now?' stage and option (d) describes the 'What is the vision?' stage (8.4.3 Figure 8.2)

5 d – A critical success factor is something that must happen if a process, project plan or service is to succeed. Metrics are used to measure the achievement of each CSF (8.4.5.2).

CHAPTER 9 (SERVICE MANAGEMENT TECHNOLOGY)

1   b – Option (4) would be a technology requirement that would support Service Operation and Continual Service Improvement as it refers to live services (9.1)

2   c – All the other options are used by IT: option (a) is used to populate or verify CMS data, option (b) is used to control the user's desktop and option (d) is used to create and use diagnostic scripts to assist with early diagnosis of incidents (9.1).

CHAPTER 12 (SAMPLE ITIL VERSION 3 FOUNDATION EXAMINATION)

1   b – Option (a) only refers to the calculation of a monetary value, option (c) refers to utility and warranty as a distracter, and (d) is one of the objectives for Demand Management (4.5.2.1)

2   c – More closely aligned service levels would be the value that Service Level Management would add (7.5.4.2)

3   c – This is an activity that would be carried out within the process of Supplier Management (5.5.2.3)

4   c – We would certainly not expect to see an incident ticket raised as part of the output of change (6.5.2.3 Figure 6.5)

5   d – Option (a) refers to utility, and options (b) and (c) refer to other value attributes, but none is associated with Demand Management (4.5.1.2)

6   c – Option 4 is an objective for Problem Management (7.6.1.2)

7   c – In option (a) the Service Desk is responsible for the incident throughout its lifecycle, in option (b) the Service Level Manager is responsible for the day-to-day service, and in option (d) the Process Owner is accountable for a specific process (2.2.5)

8   b – The validation that a service will meet business requirements before deployment falls in the Service Transition lifecycle phase (6.1)

9   b – Option (a) describes the UC and OLA with the wrong and opposite meanings to the correct answer, option (c) is inaccurate as both OLAs and UCs would have measurements set against them to determine performance in support of the SLA, and option (d) suggests both are the same type of agreements (5.5.2.2 definition of OLA: an agreement between an IT service provider and another part of the same organization to support the delivery of the services; UC: a contract between an IT service provider and a third party)

10 c – Options (a) and (b) are the outputs from the Service Design stage, and option (d) is inaccurate as the solution should be designed to accommodate the business process (5.4.1)

11 b – Option (a) suggests that it is only a planning tool, options (c) and (d) refer to Financial Management objectives (4.4.3 definition: justification for a significant item of expenditure that includes information about costs, benefits, options, issues, risks and possible problems)

12 c – Option (a) refers to 'Do', option (b) refers to 'Check' and option (d) refers to 'Act' (8.4.2)

13 a – In option (b) IT Operations provides the monitoring and control activities, in option (c) Incident Management is a process, and in option (d) Application Management provides the technical knowledge and expertise related to the applications (7.6.2.1)

14 c – Option 3 is not a type of Service Desk, as the operations bridge is part of IT Operations (7.6.1.3)

15 d – Options (a) and (c) describe the definition of maintainability, and option (b) describes the definition of serviceability (5.5.5.2 definition: a measure of how long a Configuration Item or IT Service can perform to its agreed function without interruption)

16 d – Option (a) refers to the request fulfilment process, option (b) refers to the generic RFC for all changes and option (c) refers to normal changes that should go through a formal approval process usually via the CAB (6.5.2.2)

17 a – Option (b) describes the configuration model, option (c) describes the DML in all but the fact that it is not a media library that has not passed QA, and in option (d) backups would not be stored in the DML (6.5.3.2 definition: one or more locations in which the definitive and approved versions of all software CIs are securely stored; the DML may also contain associated CIs such as licences and documentation)

18 c – This is the correct stage where we can use our knowledge from some of the experiences we have gained, as well as from the analysis of the information (6.5.4.2)

19 b – Option (a) on 'consult' is where people's opinions are sought, and options (c) and

(d) are not words used in the RACI model (2.2.3.2)

20 a – Options (b) and (c) show some of the objectives of CSI but they are narrow in their scope, and option (d) is an objective for Service Design (8.1)

21 d – All of the stated elements form part of a process as well as procedures, work instructions, triggers, input, output, capabilities etc. (2.2.4)

22 d – All options would be appropriate options for automation (9.2)

23 d – A Process Owner is always accountable for their process; other groups would take responsibility (2.2.4)

24 b – It is Application Management that would manage applications throughout their lifecycle (7.5.1.1)

25 a – Option (b) refers to the escalation of an incident up the management chain if further people need to be made aware of the incident, for option (c) incidents do not become problems just because the Service Desk cannot fix them, and in option (d) an incident should not be closed just because it cannot be fixed by the Service Desk or because the OLA is just about to be breached! (7.5.2.3 definition: transferring an incident, problem or change to a technical team with a higher level of expertise to assist)

26 b – Option (a) describes the internal teams as they relate to an OLA, and therefore the Supplier Management process would not cover this, option (c) is incorrect because it is the supplier's responsibility to justify changes required so they themselves would sit on a

CAB, and option (d) is a very narrow part of the process role (5.5.3.1)

27 c – Option 2 would fall under the Change Management process and should be raised via an RFC (7.5.3.2)

28 b – Facilities Management sits within IT Operations (7.6.3.1)

29 c – The Service Design Package should be produced during the design stage for new, changed and removed services, and as the final output into Service Transition. A Service Design Package is normally only produced for major changes (5.4.1.1)

30 a – The Service Strategy book ensures that the organization is making the right choices on behalf of and with its organization (4.1)

31 b – ITIL is a framework of good practice. Option (a) implies the international standard ISO/IEC 20000, where organizations wish to have their Service Management capabilities audited and certified; option (c) is incorrect because the IT Service Management certifications and diplomas owned by OGC and managed by APM Group form an example of a Qualification Scheme; and option (d) is incorrect because ITIL is not a methodology, it is a framework which needs to be adapted by each organization (2.3 definition: a set of best-practice guidance for IT Service Management)

32 d – All of the technology examples would help with efficiency and effectiveness during the Service Operation phase of the lifecycle (9.1)

33 d – This is the correct sequence for the Incident Management process flow (7.5.2.3)

34 a – Option (b) is incorrect because Financial Management and Supplier Management would be the only ones to consider the impact of risk, option (c) describes much more reactive dynamic processes, and in option (d) these are not processes but lifecycle phases (6.5.2.1)

35 c – In option (a) Access Management would not grant access at all times, it would very much be determined on the availability requirements that have been agreed with the business; option (b) describes the objective of information security; and option (d) describes the objective of IT Service Continuity (7.5.5.1)

36 b – The answer to the question 'Where are we now?' involves ensuring that we have an understanding of the current performance status, which is achieved through the use of baseline assessments (8.4.3 Figure 8.2)

37 b – Good Service Design is dependent on all four answers: Partners, Products, Processes and People (5.4.2)

38 c – The Application Management function needs to understand the business process in order to help identify functional and manageability requirements for application software (7.6.4.1)

39 a – Options (b) and (c) describe warranty, and option (d) is a rather generic statement for both utility and warranty combined (2.1.3 definition: functionality offered by a product or service to meet a particular need; utility is often summarized as 'what it does')

40 a – The Service Portfolio acts as the connection point or the 'spine' of all

five stages in the Service Lifecycle and is determined in Service Strategy (4.4.1).

Note: definitions source – ITIL V3 Glossary v0 1 of 30 May 2007.

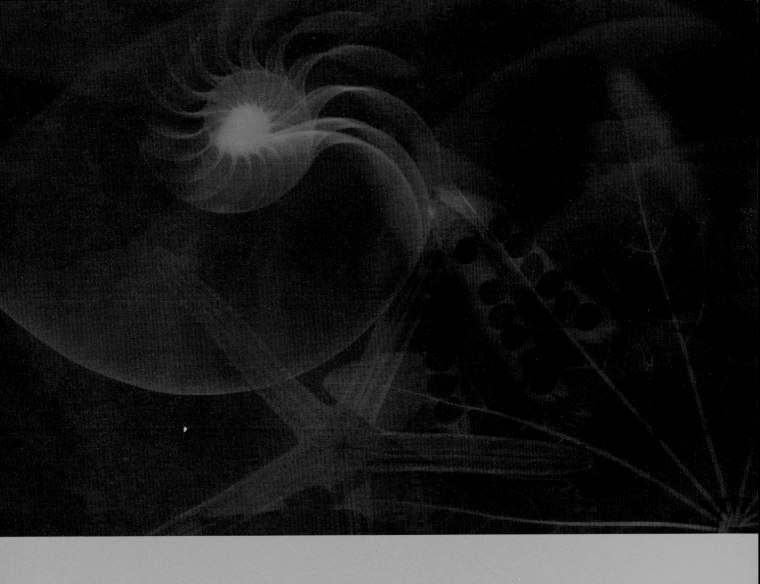

Further information

Further information

THE OFFICIAL ITIL SERVICE MANAGEMENT PRACTICES FRAMEWORK

Service Strategy (ISBN: 9780113310456)

Service Design (ISBN: 9780113310470)

Service Transition (ISBN: 9780113310487)

Service Operation (ISBN: 9780113310463)

Continual Service Improvement
(ISBN: 9780113310494)

Key Element Guide Service Strategy
(ISBN: 9780113310708)

Key Element Guide Service Design
(ISBN: 9780113310715)

Key Element Guide Service Transition
(ISBN: 9780113310722)

Key Element Guide Service Operation
(ISBN: 9780113310739)

Key Element Guide Continual Service Improvement
(ISBN: 9780113310746)

Official Introduction to the ITIL Service Lifecycle
(ISBN: 9780113310616)

ITIL V3 Foundation Handbook
(ISBN: 9780113311972)

ISO/IEC 20000 PUBLICATIONS

A Manager's Guide to Service Management. 2nd edition (updated for BS ISO/IEC 20000) (ISBN: 0580479226)

BS ISO/IEC 20000-1:2005 IT Service Management – Part 1: Specification (ISBN: 0580475298)

BS ISO/IEC 20000-2:2005 IT Service Management – Part 2: Code of Practice (ISBN: 0580475301)

IT Service Management A Self-assessment Workbook (BIP 0015-2005) (ISBN: 0580479234)

BS ISO/IEC 27001:2005(E) (BS 7799-2:2005) Information technology – security techniques – Information Security Management systems – requirements

BS ISO/IEC 17799:2005 (BS 7799-1:2005) Information technology – security techniques – code of practice for Information Security Management

USEFUL WEBSITES

ITIL

www.best-management-practice.com

www.itil-officialsite.com

Certification

www.apmgroup.co.uk

ISO/IEC 20000

www.isoiec20000certification.com

*it*SMF International

www.itsmf.org

Index

Index